THE HIGH TECH MARKETING MACHINE

Applying the
POWER OF COMPUTERS
to Out-Smart
the Competition

Timothy W. Powell

PROBUS PUBLISHING COMPANY
Chicago, Illinois
Cambridge, England

© 1993, Probus Publishing Company

ALL RIGHTS RESERVED. No part of this publication may be reproduced, stored in a retrieval system, or transmitted, in any form or by any means, electronic, mechanical, photocopying, recording, or otherwise, without the prior written permission of the publisher and the author.

This publication is designed to provide accurate and authoritative information in regard to the subject matter covered. It is sold with the understanding that the author and the publisher are not engaged in rendering legal, accounting, or other professional service.

Authorization to photocopy items for internal or personal use, or the internal or personal use of specific clients, is granted by PROBUS PUBLISHING COMPANY, provided that the U.S. $7.00 per page fee is paid directly to Copyright Clearance Center, 27 Congress Street, Salem, MA 01970, USA; Phone: 1-508-744-3350. For those organizations that have been granted a photocopy license by CCC, a separate system of payment has been arranged. The fee code for users of the Transactional Reporting Service is 1-55738-439-8/93/$00.00 + $7.00.

ISBN 1-55738-439-8

Printed in the United States of America

BB

1 2 3 4 5 6 7 8 9 0

TAQ

Probus books are available at quantity discounts when purchased for business, educational, or sales promotional use. For more information, please call the Director, Corporate / Institutional Sales at (800) 998-4644, or write:

Director, Corporate / Institutional Sales
Probus Publishing Company
1925 N. Clybourn Avenue
Chicago, IL 60614
PHONE (800) 998-4644   *FAX* (312) 868-6250

For my parents, Kay and Jim,
who by example taught me
to value words

CONTENTS

Preface   vii
Acknowledgments   ix

Part I   Introduction

Chapter 1	Introduction	3
Chapter 2	The Marketing Machine	13

Part II   The Technology Toolbox

Chapter 3	Word Processing	23
Chapter 4	Mailing List Managers	31
Chapter 5	Desktop Publishing	39
Chapter 6	Fax	47
Chapter 7	Voice Mail	55
Chapter 8	Time Managers	63
Chapter 9	Contact Managers	69
Chapter 10	Sales Force Automation	75
Chapter 11	Mapping Software	83
Chapter 12	Electronic Mail	91
Chapter 13	Groupware	99
Chapter 14	Presentation Software	107
Chapter 15	Spreadsheets	113
Chapter 16	Online Databases	121

Chapter 17	Survey Software	135
Chapter 18	Database Managers	141
Chapter 19	Scanner Data Analysis	149
Chapter 20	Multimedia	153
Chapter 21	Project Managers and Timekeepers	159
Chapter 22	Other Software	165

Part III Applying the Tools

Chapter 23	A Day in the Life	179
Chapter 24	The Value of Information	187
Chapter 25	The Future	197
Chapter 26	Where Do We Go from Here?	207

Index 217

PREFACE

If you're reading this in the computer section of a bookstore, glance at the books to the immediate left and right of this one. Chances are they're about a particular computer application (WordPerfect, PageMaker, etc.), as are the great majority of computer books. Many of these books are great as what they are—previews of the software, tutorials that help you learn to use it, and reference books to keep around while you're using it.

This book is different. It is about more than a particular software package, or even a whole category of software, such as word processing. This book covers a closely related group of business functions—sales, marketing and business development—and demonstrates how computers and other information technology can be used to enhance them. It puts business problems first, then offers solutions through technology.

This book results from my own expeditions through the technology jungles during the past decade. I hope it serves to guide you in yours.

I've given illustrations throughout of ways in which these kinds of software are being used. These are taken from both the trade press and from my own experience as a computer user and consultant.

ACKNOWLEDGMENTS

There are many individuals who either indirectly or directly assisted me in the development of this book. First I'd like to thank those people who *indirectly* helped me by providing encouragement and inspiration along the way:

Dr. George Witt, a clinical psychologist in New Haven, CT, and my first boss. George was the first person to encourage me to write—by paying me to!

Carole Congram, an author and now an independent marketing consultant, who first encouraged me to begin public speaking and writing on marketing topics, and who had a direct hand in getting some of my early work published.

Bruce W. Marcus, also an author and a marketing consultant, who first gave me a place to write on technology in marketing, and who is one of the most technology-literate people I know. Bruce is editor of *The Marcus Letter on Professional Services Marketing,* and encouraged me to write this book.

Don Welsch, a consulting economist with Jonas & Welsch, whom I've worked with in many capacities for nearly 15 years. Don's budget bought me my first computer, and later Don introduced me to the joys of the Macintosh.

Julio Herrera, a portfolio manager with Reiger, Robinson and Harrington, who first convinced me of the power of computers in a marketing environment—and answered lots of my stupid questions.

Janet Coolick, Vice President at Shearson, Lehman Brothers, with whom I've had many enlightening discussions of some of the topics presented herein.

Steven Bash and Howard Bleiwas, both independent consultants and brilliant technologists, who live on the leading edge.

Jim Shanahan of Business Dynamics, a master marketer, who is always full of pragmatic insights about the role of technology.

Then there are those who *directly* assisted me in the preparation of this book:

Marlene Chamberlain, my lead editor at Probus, who believed in this project from the start, and was able to convince others of its value. All of the production and editorial people I dealt with at Probus were first-rate and contributed substantially to the quality of this book.

The software publishers mentioned in this book, many of whom sent me review copies of their products and spoke with me.

Finally, there are the people who give me the emotional *support* that any sustained creative undertaking demands:

Ellen Matson, my lifemate, who provided suggestions, support, hot tea, and back rubs during my six months of writing this book.

And finally, the lights of my life, my sons Michael Powell and David Powell, who constantly remind me that computers can also be used purely to have fun!

PART ONE

INTRODUCTION

Chapter One

Introduction

Reading this chapter will help you decide whether this book can help you in your business. It will tell you what I've tried to accomplish in this book, and specifically what is *not* covered. Many of the chapters are organized along the same basic structure, and here I'll describe that structure.

Then, I'll suggest the next steps to follow if a software package or class seems to be of potential value. Finally, if you're about to buy a new computer, I'll suggest how to go about evaluating some of the many options available.

Is This Book for You?

This book has several distinct audiences:

- *Marketing and sales professionals.* People in larger organizations who are responsible for marketing, sales, and business development. Personal computers have made large inroads here, but are still primarily used for word processing.
- *Entrepreneurs.* People who own or operate their own businesses. The small business is one of the fastest-growing markets for personal computers. Using information technology effectively is a key to controlling the overhead of a fledgling organization.
- *Independents.* People who work out of their own offices, often at home. Due to the massive downsizing of American businesses, many talented managers are making their livings as independent consultants. According to a recent survey, there are 23 million people working in home offices. These people need

computers to help them compete effectively with larger organizations.
- *Senior executives.* Large-company MIS managers and middle-market CEOs who want to be sure they are getting the most out of all the investments they've recently made in new information technologies. I hope many "Have we tried this?" dialogues will result from this book.
- *Nonprofit marketers.* Fundraisers for charitable organizations and political campaigns. Many of the techniques here will apply equally well in public sector and nonprofit organizations.

Particularly attracted to this book will be the baby-boom managers now coming into positions of leadership. Many of these managers are already comfortable with information technology, and presumably many of the ideas here will be familiar to them. This group is eager to explore new applications that have bottom-line impacts.

Technology neophytes in the audience should not be discouraged—I was one myself less than a decade ago. Bear in mind the historical perspective. We're still near the very beginning of the age of electronic information, which began around 1950. No one has that great a head start, and there's no better time than now to begin to learn about it.

What Is This Book Trying to Accomplish?

The main objective of *The High-Tech Marketing Machine* is to show how computers are being used as revenue generators both in corporate and entrepreneurial environments. It is "how to" oriented and saves the reader time and effort in selecting the right tool for the job.

Real-world case studies and examples of computer applications are cited throughout. These are taken both from my personal experience as an applications developer and from a clippings file on the topic that I have been building for several years.

This book is written in English, not computerese. The tone is readable, straightforward, and nontechnical. Where a technical term is really needed, I have defined that term in nontechnical language. The book is written to address the needs of DOS, Windows and Macintosh users at all levels of expertise.

What Is Not Included in This Book?

A note on what this book is not. This book is not a primer on the operations of a personal computer. There are no chapters here on how to turn on a computer, or what a hard disk drive is. I have assumed that you, the reader, have a basic knowledge of computer operations, appropriate to whichever computer platform you're using. If you don't, there are books, classes, and self-instruction audiotapes and videotapes to get you started. (Please buy this book now anyway—so you can get a head start on these business-generating ideas.)

Nor have I set out to include *all* types of software that are useful to the business professional. For example, there is nothing here about financial management or accounting software, both of which are critical to the success of a business enterprise (and even to households.)

Likewise, there is nothing here about utility software, the very useful software that makes it easier to keep other software running smoothly. These include file backup and recovery tools, hard disk maintenance and organization tools, screen dimmers, power conservation for laptops and notebooks, virus trappers, and so on. Again, there are other sources that cover these types of applications.

How Is This Book Organized?

This book is organized into three large parts:

- **Introduction** (Chapters 1 and 2). This forms the prologue to the book's layout and the ideas contained in it.
- **The Technology Toolbox** (Chapters 3 through 22). This is the heart of the book. Each of these chapters describes a set of information tools.
- **Applying the Tools** (Chapters 23 through 26). These chapters discuss how to apply and evaluate the tools. Chapter 23 is basically a cross-reference to the rest of the book. It starts from the point of view of the marketing problems that need solving, then directs you back to the chapters that describe technologies that may help.

Most of the chapters in the second part are organized into parallel sections. This will enable you to quickly get at the information you need about a particular class of software. These sections are described below.

Basic Description of the Software

This section describes briefly the basic capabilities of most software in this class. It will give you a general idea of what the software does.

Benefits of the Software

This section tells you, if you do begin using the software and use it well enough to realize its potential, what benefits you should expect from it.

Marketing and Sales Applications

This describes examples of how this type of software is being (or could be) used in a marketing or sales context.

You may be able to decide from these first three sections whether it's worth looking further into this type of software.

Case Study or Example

Where available I've included a description of one or more "real-world" installations of the software, and exactly how it is being used. Some of these case studies I've gathered from the business press over the past several years. Others come out of my personal experiences as a database developer and software consultant.

What to Look For

Among a particular category of software, there usually are key points that differentiate among various packages available. This section will enable you to enter the software marketplace with the ability to distinguish among them. Unfortunately, there is usually no single program that best serves the needs of all users. This section is designed to help you determine which software is right for you.

Profile of One Package

We then take a closer look at one leading package in the category being described. This is partly done to further illustrate the functions of the whole class of software, and partly to provide a benchmark against which other software can be measured.

Introduction 7

Some of the packages I've profiled here are from the large software publishers—Microsoft, Lotus Development, and Borland International, for example. Others are from companies you may have never heard of. Each package has generally been received positively in the trade, and to my knowledge they are all commercially available, either through software retailers or directly from the publishers.

Major Packages

Finally, there is a table that lists major packages in the class for the three major personal computer operating environments—DOS, Macintosh, and Windows. I have not included OS/2, UNIX, or other more esoteric environments, as there aren't many applications for them related to marketing.

The publisher of each package is listed, along with its address and phone number. Toll-free numbers have been listed where available. List prices of the software have not been included, since often these do not reflect the actual prices being charged by software superstores and direct mail retailers. No warranty is implied herein about the features contained in each package, which can of course change periodically as new versions are released.

Company names and the names of software packages and other proprietary products listed herein are trademarks owned by their respective publishers and manufacturers.

What Do You Do Next?

Suppose after reading a chapter of this book, you are introduced to a new class of software that you think would be useful in developing your business? What then?

I have included at the end of each chapter a list of the leaders in the class of software. This is *not* a comprehensive list, and in fact may not include the software package that ends up being best for you. However, the packages I have included are among the best established, and serve to illustrate many of the features of the class of software.

As a next step, I'd recommend getting more information on those packages. Here are three ways to do that:

- *Call the manufacturer.* Phone numbers are included here for that reason. Each software publisher will send you a sales brochure on the software. Also included may be recent reviews of the package. Sometimes there is also a free or inexpensive demo disk they can send you.
- *Try the software.* If you have a colleague who uses the software, or a very nice local software dealer, test drive a full version of the software.
- *Buy a book.* If you are unable to actually use the software before you buy it, a good book dedicated to the latest version of the package may give you valuable insights. An investment of $20 to $30 in a book may save you time and money later. These books can be found in most large bookstores and computer stores.

You may find that the general category of software seems appropriate for you, but for whatever reasons, the particular package I've profiled here doesn't work for you. In that case, you'll have to do some more research. The major mass market computer magazines periodically review whole classes of software, giving detailed information about the features, performance, and prices of each. They'll probably be available in your local library. My favorites are *PC Magazine* (Ziff-Davis) for IBM compatibles, and *Mac User* (Ziff-Davis) for the Macintosh.

Computer trade magazines are also very helpful. Their reviews often include excerpts from interviews conducted with users of the software. These magazines are generally available only to people in the industry, but you may find them in some libraries. They include *PC Week* (Ziff-Davis), *Mac Week* (Ziff-Davis), and *InfoWorld* (IDG.)

After you do make a purchase, give yourself some time to get comfortable with the software. Publishers' claims notwithstanding, it is the rare program that can be used effectively right out of the package. It will take some time to figure out how the software works before you can customize it to work the way you do (not the way the software author thinks you do). Be patient!

Which Platform Should You Choose?

Throughout this book I have describe software for IBM compatible machines as well as the Macintosh. In the event you haven't selected a platform for your "marketing machine," this section briefly describes the advantages of each.

First, please bear in mind that when you choose hardware, you're also choosing an operating environment. When you choose an IBM compatible machine, in effect you're limited to DOS, Windows, or OS/2. (There are some other operating systems, but there's not much software written for them.) Most IBM compatible machines sold today are equipped to run Windows.

Conversely, you need an Apple Macintosh to run the Mac Operating System. The rumor that a version may be developed for IBM compatibles is so far only that.

The second key thing to keep in mind is that your first consideration should be which software will do what you want it to do. Then you'll need to get the machine to run that software. So-called "killer applications" (the ones we end up not being able to live without) often drive hardware sales. Many early IBM machines were bought in order to run Lotus 1-2-3, just as many Macintoshes were bought to run Aldus PageMaker.

Just to set the record straight, I use both IBM compatibles and Macintoshes, depending on the task at hand.

Graphic User Interfaces

The choice between IBM compatible and Macintosh machines used to mean a choice between a "text-based" user interface (IBM) and a graphic user interface (GUI). With the introduction of the graphics-based Windows and OS/2 for IBMs, this is no longer true.

There is no reason today not to take advantage of the graphic interface. The early objections of purists that they slow the machine down simply do not apply to today's blazing hardware. Studies by the market researcher Temple, Barker & Sloane[1] have indicated that GUI users find these advantages over non-GUI users:

- Greater productivity
- Fewer mistakes

- Less frustration
- Less fatigue

If you are already running certain DOS software, and can't or don't choose to upgrade, don't worry. Graphics-ready machines can still run older software that doesn't take advantage of graphic capabilities.

Advantages of IBM Compatibles

IBM compatible machines have these key advantages over the Macintosh:

- *Many vendors.* The great majority of IBM compatibles are *not* made by IBM, but rather by quality "clone" makers, such as Dell and Gateway 2000. This creates healthy competition, and lots of options for the buyer.
- *Price.* Because of the intense competition among these suppliers, the recent price war has driven both manufacturing and retail margins very low. Prices of even the most powerful machines are very attractive, even for home-office buyers.
- *Larger installed base.* Current figures put the installed base of IBM compatibles at over 80 percent of the entire microcomputer base. This generally results in greater availability of software, technical support, and peer advice.
- *Greater software selection.* Because developers are aware of this installed base balance, they develop most applications first for the IBM compatible. They may then "port" the program to the Macintosh, but this generally happens six months to a year later.

Advantages of the Macintosh

Nevertheless, there are substantial reasons why Apple Computer continues to thrive, while IBM flounders. Many of these have to do with the inherent advantages of the Macintosh:

- *Better user interface.* The Mac's version of the graphic interface, though similar to the IBM's running under Windows, is more evolved and easier to use. Most of the applications pro-

grams, even from different manufacturers, conform to the same basic set of command conventions. This means greater productivity and ease of use.
- *Better file management.* It's generally easier to name, organize, move, and maintain documents and other files with the Macintosh.
- *Better memory management.* Many modern programs are designed to work substantially faster with larger amounts of main memory (RAM). It is generally easier to set up a "loaded" Macintosh than an equivalent IBM compatible.
- *Built-in networking.* The Macintosh is ready to do basic networking out of the box, while the IBM compatible requires additional hardware cards and software.
- *Built-in multimedia.* Many Macs are multimedia-ready out of the box, while again most IBM compatibles require additional hardware.
- *Better laptops.* Apple leapfrogged all manufacturers of IBM compatible laptops with its introduction of the PowerBook series. Even confirmed IBM compatible users often prefer PowerBooks, mainly because of the sensational clarity of their screens.

Coming Soon: Interoperability

Interoperability is computer jargon for the ability to run any software on any computer. At this point, in the real world this is limited to the ability of Macs and IBMs to share files created by some software and to co-exist on the same networks. The convergence of the platforms will continue, with more and more software being developed using core code that enables it to run on either machine.

True interoperability will come in the next generation of PCs. Apple and IBM have joint ventures to develop both the hardware and the operating system software to make this happen.

In other words, before long the whole question of alternative platforms will most likely be a nonissue.

A Note on Nomenclature

Finally, a note on how I've used some terms herein.

- *Data/Information/Intelligence.* To a certain extent, I use these terms interchangeably. To the extent there is a distinction, it's toward a progressive level of analysis, organization, and communication of findings.
- *Product/Service.* Because this book is targeted at both service and product marketers, I have used either or both terms. Please feel free to substitute whatever it is that you're selling.
- *Marketing/Sales.* Much of what I discuss here applies to both of these closely related activities, and therefore distinctions aren't drawn. Where they need to be, I'd say that marketing supports sales—and only sales pays our salaries.

Endnote

1. Lisa Day-Copeland, "Clinical Research Finds PC Users Are More Productive with GUI Interface," *PC Week,* July 23, 1990: 142.

Chapter Two

The Marketing Machine

Some business functions benefited early from computer technology. As early as the 1960s, finance and operations began to be transformed by this technology. One cannot imagine a business of *any* size running its accounts on ledger paper or projecting its cash flow needs using oversized paper worksheets.

Similarly, shop floor operations are today dominated by computer technology. Scheduling of personnel, determination of the amount of raw materials needed at a particular time, and the actual control of physical machine functions are all accomplished by computers.

Marketers Discover Computers

It was not until the late 1980s that marketing managers began to take advantage of computers and related information technology. This is ironic, in view of the fact that marketing and sales comprise some of the most information- and communications-intensive functions of the modern corporation. This lag probably has something to do with the corporate culture of marketers—their training, their corporate role models, and so on.

But marketers have discovered computers, and they're not about to go back to the way things used to be. Marketing and sales applications are the areas most frequently mentioned by corporate managers for future development by their Management Information Systems (MIS) departments.

The introduction of the personal computer in the early 1980s brought the information revolution out of the air-conditioned glass-walled rooms of the MIS departments. Information consumers could—at last—get their hands, quite literally, on the information needed to guide their businesses strategically.

The trend toward end-user computing has continued unabated, prompted in some cases by refinements in the technology itself. For example, the recent introduction of laptop computers has added even more fuel to businesses' appetites for applications in marketing and sales.

As Professor Warren McFarlan of Harvard Business School has said, "Information technology changes the way you compete."[1] Things will never be the same.

The Theme of This Book

Corporate MIS staffers often can't keep up with the demand for new competitive applications. Maintaining existing applications usually absorbs most of their resources. End users are left to fend for themselves. They often end up reinventing the wheel, at great cost to themselves and the companies they work for.

This book is designed to help. It is a marketing manager's guidebook through the technology jungle. Its basic premise is as follows:

Microcomputer technology, intelligently deployed and applied, can pay for itself—many times over—by taking on the repetitive, drudge aspects of marketing and business development.

The manager is freed to concentrate on the real mind work of marketing strategy and tactics.

By marketing manager, I am including anyone who has marketing, sales, or business development as a significant part—but not necessarily all—of his or her responsibilities. This, of course, includes both the entrepreneur and the individual practitioner.

Personal computers are extremely flexible machines. As I will show in a moment, they can be made to replace any of a number of other office technologies. Yet many personal computers are used mainly for word processing. This is a holdover from their legacy as replacements for typewriters, but it unnecessarily limits our view of the utility of office computers.

The Untapped Potential

Getting information technology to live up to its potential is one of the greatest challenges facing corporate technology managers. In fact *anyone* who uses a computer in their daily activities faces this challenge, whether knowingly or not.

Most business computers currently are under-used assets. They are simply not pulling their weight in many areas, particularly in developing new business. In spite of the great proliferation of this hardware during the 1980s, most measures of white-collar work force productivity are flat or declining.

It's not the computers' fault, they're just tools. It's *our* fault, the great body of users. Okay, let's not be too hard on ourselves. Let's admit computers were at first fun toys to play with. Then, when we really tried to make them work, we found that—well, let's just say the advertisements for technology often outdistanced *by far* what was typically feasible on a regular basis in a demanding business setting.

Computers are doing better. They can learn to do even *better*. They learn very fast, given the right software. Computers *must* do better if we are to regain and retain our business competitiveness in global markets.

Properly equipped, computers can be fashioned into "marketing machines," able to support nearly any marketing program. This book shows you how to build a customized marketing machine, using existing, commercially available hardware and software.

The "machine" is a metaphor for the repetitive, drudge aspects of every marketer's job that are often better done by a computer. With staff reductions what they've been lately, often having human assistance is no longer even an option. Every marketer must learn to work smarter. Computers are low-cost assistants in the marketing wars.

Flexibility

One of the things that makes computers so valuable is that they are the ultimate chameleons—they can become whatever the user wants them to become, depending on the kind of software that is being operated. They can assist, emulate—and sometimes replace—many other kinds of office technology.

Computer Technology	Office Technology Replaced
Word processing	Typewriter
Electronic mail	Telephone
Desktop presentation	Slide projector
Desktop publishing	Typesetting machine
Desktop publishing	Paste-up board
Contact manager	Rolodex
Fax board	Fax machine
Voice mail	Answering machine

The Marketing Information System Vision

Computers can help sales and marketing professionals in a number of ways. I'll outline two similar expert views on the subject, worth bearing in mind as you read the rest of the book.

The Academic View

Professors John Burch and Gary Grudnitski[2] lay out this description of what functions an ideal marketing information system should support.

- *Sales force management and support.* Gives front line troops access to information about quantities of products on hand, pricing and promotions, status of invoices and back orders, delivery dates, product specifications. Helps them process orders. Replaces paperwork, including call reports. Gives them information on leads. Tracks customer information, including objections to the sale.
- *Sales performance analysis and forecasting.* Sales and profitability by region, salesperson, customer, product line, and so on. Includes comparisons to previous periods and the industry as a whole.
- *Marketing research and intelligence.* Includes analysis of data produced from point-of-sale UPC (Universal Product Code) scanners, primary research data from CATI (Computer-Assisted Telephone Interviewing) systems, and electronic mapping of sales and target data.

- *Product analysis and strategy.* Includes test-market data; new product reports; reports comparing various pricing and promotional strategies; analyses of product mix; and reports that track a product over its life cycle.
- *Promotion.* This includes information on advertising, sales promotion, and public relations budgets; the effectiveness of each of these activities; and media selection based on cost per thousand delivered messages.
- *Customer service and analysis.* This includes Electronic Data Interchange (EDI) for direct entry of orders, product and price information available to customers, technical support, customer activity and profitability, and customer complaint tracking and follow-up.
- *Budgeting.* Including budgets for sales force management and support, market research, promotions and advertising. May also include logistics and distribution, although typically this is outside the direct control of the marketing and sales functions.

The Consultants' View

The Index Group of Cambridge, MA, a leading consulting firm in the applications of technology to marketing and sales, has proposed a similar outline of technology support for marketing.[3]

- *Market intelligence system.* Includes customer profiles, market tracking, decision support, trend monitoring, and cross-selling information.
- *Target marketing system.* Includes database marketing, telemarketing, niche/regional marketing, and profitability analysis.
- *Dealer system.* Includes marketing support, sales support, business management support, and communications to and from dealers.
- *Sales system.* Includes field office communications, account management, sales support, point-of-sale systems, and prospecting systems.
- *Delivery system.* Includes Electronic Data Interchange (EDI), demand forecasting, inventory management, order entry and fulfillment, and invoicing modules.

- *Customer support system.* Includes customer communications, customer satisfaction, service and support, training and customer education, and product/service enhancements.

How to Use These Theoretical Models

I think it's helpful to keep these two models in mind. They're both excellent, and similar, theoretical models for the applications of computer technology in marketing. They can help you audit your own use of information in marketing your company's products and services. They provide functional guidelines, at a macro level, for applications of information technology.

My approach in this book has been more hands-on. I have reviewed low-cost, available technologies and described some of their applications in marketing. The central idea is that using these existing tools, a garden-variety personal computer can be transformed into a "marketing machine" with many of the same features of much more elaborate, expensive, custom-designed and custom-coded systems.

Not only are these lower-cost implementations of the marketing information systems vision interesting simply because they are lower-cost, they are often *more functional* at the same time. They allow the end user—the salesperson or the marketing manager—to *get the information he or she needs, when he or she needs it, in a format he or she can use.* These, by the way, are some of the key criteria by which the value and utility of information systems are typically judged.

Inbound and Outbound Applications

Finally, it's important to keep in mind two fundamentally different ways to use information in marketing: inbound and outbound applications.

Inbound applications are those that consume information. Included here are both applications that consume information *internal* to the organization (like accounting records) and those that consumer information from *outside* the organization (like using information from a database to research a potential client). Usually the goal here is to reduce uncertainty in some way. The end result is greater efficiency and effectiveness of the sales or marketing function.

Outbound applications are those that produce, or at least distribute, information. Information is used as a value-added adjunct to whatever core service or product is being sold. Home banking by phone is a good example. The core service (banking) is enhanced by the technology to deliver it directly to the customer's home.

Strategies to arrive at these applications are essentially different. We arrive at *inbound* applications by asking, "What information do we need to sell or market smarter?" We arrive at *outbound* applications by asking, "What information do our customers need to make their lives easier (and in particular, to make buying our products and services easier)?"

They're both equally valuable and productive approaches. Designing inbound applications requires us to look at how we operate, and how these operations can be enhanced or developed. Please note that the best computer applications come not from simply *automating* an existing process, but from *rethinking* and *redesigning* the process, sometimes from the ground up. (*Re-engineering* is the current buzzword for this.)

Designing outbound applications requires us to look more closely at our customers and prospects, and how they use (or could use) information provided by us. They come to depend on information we provide, and this can create a lasting business advantage.

Monitoring the competition in this regard is also important. A competitor's outbound information application can sometimes pre-empt your own.

But enough theory—let's begin our tour through these new technologies and their applications to marketing.

Endnotes

1. F. Warren McFarlan, "Information Technology Changes the Way You Compete," *Strategy* (Boston: Harvard Business School Press, 1991.)

2. John Burch and Gary Grundnitski, *Information Systems: Theory and Practice—Fifth Edition* (New York: Wiley, 1989.)

3. Dennis Eskow, "Channel Systems Put PCs on Front Line," *PC Week,* March 5, 1990: 135-136.

PART TWO

THE TECHNOLOGY TOOLBOX

Chapter Three

Word Processing

Let's start with that most ubiquitous of software applications the word processor. The true potential of this software in marketing and sales is often overlooked.

Basic Description of Word Processing Software

Word processing software has virtually replaced the typewriter in modern business. It enables us to make changes quickly and easily. In particular we can perform the following functions:

- *Formatting words.* Making our words look nice—as good as they do in a typeset print document—is easy with a word processor. Each typeface can be specified, often from a wide range of possibilities. Type size can be selected. Type style (bold, italics, and so on) can be selected. The leading—the amount of white space between the lines of type—can be defined. Justification—how type lines up at the margins—can be set up. Margins and tab settings can be easily set and reset. Headers and footers—the words that repeat at the top or bottom of each page—can easily be defined and changed.

    Some word processing programs include the ability to create *style sheets* that predefine all the characteristics of a particular kind of type: the font, leading, margins, justification, and so on. All of these characteristics contribute to the overall definition of a style, which is then given a name (like "body text"). If you later decide that you'd like the body text to be indented five spaces, rather than flush left, you simply redefine the style, and all occurrences of that style are automatically changed.

- *Editing.* We can pour words into a word processor without too much attention to how they're organized. The editing of our work can come after the original thought is captured. Most writers find that this is more effective than trying to pre-edit words before typing.
- *Cutting and pasting.* Most software packages allow you to open more than one file or document at the same time. This enables you to cut and paste between the two electronically—still a miracle to those of us who remember physically cutting and using rubber cement to reorganize documents.

  There are also functions that enable you to bring in a whole section of text that has been prepared in advance. This is handy where boilerplate language can be used in many circumstances, with little or no modification.
- *Electronic filing.* Many word processors include file management functions, to allow the grouping of files that are logically related. This also allows you to easily search for files that you may have misplaced.
- *Mail merging.* This feature enables you to integrate standard text with a data file of text that changes for each document. It is designed to facilitate direct mailings. We'll discuss it more below.

Add-In Functions

As word processing software has matured, there has been a tendency to provide additional functions: formerly only available as extra-cost options. These options are usually invented by third-party software developers and sold separately at first. Then they are often acquired by the word processing developer and offered at no additional cost with the main package. Finally, they are fully integrated into the main software's feature set.

- *Spelling checkers.* A spelling checker is an electronic dictionary that checks for spelling errors, provides correct spellings, and automatically hyphenates text. It is often an adaptation of an existing dictionary. Most word processing software now has this feature built in.

Some spelling checkers work in real time—as soon as a word is keyed in that the software doesn't recognize, the software beeps or offers some other warning. Others check spelling in batch mode—after the selection is typed without interruption, you go back and check the whole selection at one time.

Most spelling checkers enable you to specify words that you want to add to the electronic dictionary—your own name, for example—so that it doesn't waste your time by suggesting alternatives.

- *Outliners.* Most of us can't sit down in front of a blank page and organize our thoughts as we write. Outliners help us get started by capturing the basic structure of what we're going to say. We can work with the material in this form—reorganize it and flesh it out—before actually writing. Writing then becomes a matter of filling in the gaps and providing transitions.
- *Thesauruses.* Like spelling checkers, these are electronic equivalents of hard-copy thesauruses. They enable you to find the word with just the right meaning, and to offer variation where you've been over-using a particular word.
- *Grammar checkers.* These programs promise a level of sophistication beyond simple spell checking (although they include that feature). They check for a range of word usage errors—words accidentally repeated, sentences where the noun and verb don't match, clichés and tired phrases, active versus passive voice, and so on. They can often be configured to the writer's own style. Sometimes you can select among multiple styles, depending on what's appropriate for the document you're writing.

Most of these packages also grade your writing in terms of its clarity. This score is based on the number of syllables per word, number of words per sentence, and number of sentences per paragraph.

Most of these programs are stand-alone programs, but this technology is beginning to be incorporated into word processing software. Grammar checkers are still evolving, and have received mixed reviews to date. Some writers find their suggestion to be mechanical and inappropriate.

There is no question that one must be very careful in using these programs. Fortunately, they can't be set on automatic pilot—as yet they work only in batch mode, and they require the user's intervention at each step. This is fortunate, because many of their suggestions *are* mechanical and inappropriate.

I find, though, that some of the suggestions these packages make are worth considering, and I usually adopt between one-third and one-half of a good package's suggestions. One must know what one is doing well enough to be able to separate the usable suggestions from those that should be ignored.

- *Page layout.* Advanced software packages are now able to do what you used to need desktop publishing software to achieve. Tables can be created easily. Graphics created in other applications can be placed and sized in a word processing document, and the text can be made to "flow" around them; multiple columns of text (like in a newspaper) can be created easily.

Marketing and Sales Applications for Word Processors

There are many times we need to create and edit documents for marketing and sales purposes:

- Creating direct mail
- Writing advertising copy
- Sending follow-up letters after a personal sales call
- Writing business proposals
- Creating hand-outs and overhead transparencies for presentations and meetings
- Creating training materials

Word processing can help you look better in every one of these situations, and can save you time in doing so. In addition, computer-generated text can be considerably more persuasive than that prepared on a typewriter because the results look more professional and polished.

Mail Merge

Mail merge is a function built into most word processors that, as its name indicates, facilitates direct mailings. It enables you to create letters that are custom addressed to a series of people. Each letter is the result of merging data from a list file (your list of names) with a body text file (which contains the basic letter). Mail merge can also be used to print mailing labels.

The list of names can be created and maintained in the word processing program. This way of doing it is error prone and difficult to maintain, however, and when using mail merge I recommend that the list be maintained in a database management program, then imported to the word processor before each mailing is generated.

My experience indicates that mail merge is best suited to small mailings (fewer than 100 pieces). For anything larger than that, you will probably want to use a mailing list manager. (Such programs are discussed in Chapter 4.)

Example—A "Proposal Kit"

This example comes from close to home—my own consulting practice. I am constantly putting together proposals for consulting projects. Many times my clients want these proposals within a day. I have used word processors to make the process less time-consuming and more effective.

I first created a foundation document that contains the following:

- *The skeleton of the proposal.* The basic parts of the proposal—project objective, project approach, cost and timing, and so on—are listed as major headings.
- *Boilerplate language.* The basic terms of how we do business, our major resources and our overall qualifications, are listed. These basically do not change from proposal to proposal, though they may be modified to fit the needs of a particular client.

Separate documents contain the following:

- *Our specific qualifications.* This usually includes a list of client relationships we have in the current prospect's industry, and brief descriptions of assignments in that industry we've recently completed.

- *Key biographies.* I have consistently-formatted biographical sketches of my colleagues, each in a separate document. (Sometimes I have more than one, each of which emphasizes a particular specialty or expertise.) This enables me to describe the proposed project team very quickly.

Finally, in a separate application (a spreadsheet), I have a project budget that describes each work step, who will be assigned to it, and how much time it is expected to take. The formatting and formula relationships are set up as a template, and the particular data elements are customized for each project. This budget is linked to my proposal in such a way that if I change it during the course of discussing the project scope with the prospective client, the changes will automatically be reflected in the proposal.

Finally, I have a section I can pull into the proposal where the prospect can sign to indicate his or her acceptance of the project as proposed.

These six elements constitute a proposal kit that enables me to put out relatively high-quality proposals very quickly. The time I save can be used to think through the client's problem more carefully, and to do some preliminary research on the issue.

What to Look for in a Word Processor

- *Features.* One of the main things to consider is the presence of the add-in options listed above. If they are not in your package, you will have to buy other software to achieve the same results. In that case, you may have to deal with importing text in and out of the program—this can be time consuming, and can result in the loss of text formatting.
- *Integration with other software.* If you plan to link documents, make sure that the word processor you choose is compatible with this other application. For example, you may want to bring in data from a spreadsheet program to your document. Some combinations of programs achieve this linkage more easily than others.

  Similarly, you may want to bring graphics into your document—drawings, diagrams, or photographs. Again, this is easier in some cases than others.

- *Ease of use.* Most of us, no matter how large our software arsenal, spend more time with our word processor than all other applications combined. It must be easy to use. A graphic user interface (GUI) can be a great time saver here, as can the what-you-see-is-what-you-get capability that usually goes with it.

Profile of One Word Processing Package— Microsoft Word

This book is being prepared in Microsoft Word for the Macintosh, Version 5. I find it to be at the same time the most powerful and the most congenial word processing software. It formats words on the page very easily, and includes a *tool bar* graphic palette of the most frequently used formatting commands. It has many powerful commands not found in other software and can be extensively customized to each individual user's needs and preferences. It contains powerful spelling and grammar checkers, a thesaurus, and an outlining program.

Word can now do things that once only desktop publishing software could do. This includes creating columns of text, borders around text, and "wrapping" text around inset text or graphics.

Word pioneered the use of *style sheets*, an approach that is now being adopted by some desktop publishing software. Style sheets enable you to take all aspects of a given kind of text—typeface, style, size, indent, tab stops, justification—and define them as a style. When you want to use that style again, you just tell the program what style you're using, and type. The software formats the text just the way you want it. You can use the styles that come with the program, make up your own, or modify existing styles to create new ones.

Even after the fact, it's easy to apply a style to a piece of text, or to change the style that applies to that text. More important, you can change a style universally throughout a document. Suppose you have a style called "Subheads" that is all caps and bold, flush left, in 12-point type. After looking at your whole 50-page document, you decide it would look better if the subheads were upper/lower, centered, in 18-point type. All you have to do is redefine the style as appropriate—this takes a couple of keystrokes—and every sidehead in your document changes instantly. This near-miraculous feature can save you lots of time.

Major Word Processing Packages

	DOS	Windows	Macintosh
WordPerfect WordPerfect Corp. 1555 North Technology Way Orem, UT 84057 (800) 451-5151	●	●	●
Word Microsoft Corporation 1 Microsoft Way Redmond, WA 98052-6399 (206) 882-8080	●	●	●

Chapter Four

Mailing List Managers

Direct mail is an increasingly important part of practically any modern marketing program. This can be attributed to two major trends:

- *The fragmentation of markets.* Some pundits have announced the end of the mass market. In many areas—food, for example—consumer needs and preferences have become very diversified. Food manufacturers often produce their products in a regular version, a low-salt version, a low-fat version, and a version in an environmentally friendly package. The average supermarket now stocks three times the number of items it stocked in 1970.
- *The fragmentation of media.* During the past 20 years, the number of media outlets has proliferated, both in print and television. The number of special-interest magazines blossomed, thereby challenging the overall effectiveness of mass-appeal publications. Similarly, cable TV provides a feasible alternative for advertisers who used to have to chose from among three networks.

As a result, the importance of advertising in the overall marketing mix has diminished. The growth areas have been in promotions and in direct marketing.

A mailing list may, in fact, be among a company's most valuable assets. This is especially likely to be true if it is a service company. When a bankruptcy judge was recently assigning value to the remaining assets of the failing firm of Drexel Burnham Lambert, one of the two most valuable assets was deemed to be the firm's customer lists. (The other was its proprietary stock trading software.)

Computers are ideally suited for helping with the more mundane tasks involved in managing a mailing list of any size. The first decision to make is whether to manage the list internally, or whether to use an outside service bureau.

Outside bureaus typically use mainframe computers or minicomputers to handle a wide variety of list management functions. They may also offer letter shop functions like affixing labels, stuffing envelopes, and delivering the completed packages to the Postal Service.

If you're going to manage your list in-house, there are again two options: have your internal MIS department do it, or do it yourself. If your MIS department is equipped to do so, they may be able to provide you with the same kinds of service as an outside bureau. Cost savings may be available here, and you may be able to interface more readily with other company systems than you would with an outside vendor.

Nowadays, it's also possible to do it yourself. More and more marketers are finding it desirable to manage lists on a PC. The advantages may include better responsiveness and shorter turnarounds, better control, and greater tendency to use the list for targeted campaign-type mailings.

Basic Description of Mailing List Management Software

In terms of their flexibility and the size of lists they can handle, mailing list managers take over where mail merge functions within word processors leave off. Mailing list managers are specialized database programs optimized for managing bulk mailing lists. They allow for relatively easy updating and maintenance of the file. They typically can produce labels in several different formats, and allow various data sorts to be easily accomplished.

Mailing list managers usually include a *merge and purge* feature. This enables you to bring together various lists—including those purchased from outside vendors—and to integrate them, while at the same time eliminating duplications. Most mailing list managers include summary statistics that help you analyze your list, for example by geographic breakdown.

Mailing list managers are related to contact managers (see Chapter 9), which contain some list management functions, as well as other capabilities.

The latest variation on mailing list managers is software that combines list management functions with actual list data for prospecting. This kind of bundled product is known informally as *infoware*.

A variation on the mailing list is the *customer information file,* which merges mailing list data with account purchase histories, and which usually contains linkages to external demographic files.

Benefits of Mailing List Managers

Mailing list managers help you:

- *Control costs.* Presorting mail often results in a reduced postage rate. Eliminating duplicates reduces postage and production costs—and the irritation level of your prospects!
- *Target your messages.* The most effective direct marketing messages often are those targeted to a specific group. List software makes it easy to target messages to specific segments of your customer and prospect base. For example, the most likely buyers for a new product may be those who have previously purchased a similar product. If you have a customer database, it is easy to locate that group and mail only to them.
- *Improve the quality of your direct mail.* The ability to personalize your message, along with the ability to target those most likely to respond to it, give your direct mail a less junky quality. For example, addressing a prospect by name is preferable to a pitch that starts "Dear occupant."

Marketing and Sales Applications for Mailing List Software

Mailing list management software is optimized for marketing purposes, including:

- *Prospecting.* Mailings to potential customers can be of the general pitch variety. They are, however, most effective when a specific offer is made that is "too good to refuse."
  Specifically targeting a mailing to a particular segment of a list can also be more effective than sending a general letter. And it is generally agreed that a personalized letter is more likely to be read than one that starts "Dear sir or madam."
- *Customer contact.* It costs much more money and effort to acquire a new customer than it does to keep an existing one. Customer mailings can be used to keep them informed of new products, improvements, changes at the company, or any other items of interest. Again, a personalized approach is preferable to a generic opening.
- *Promotions.* Special offers and other promotions can be announced by mail to customers.

What to Look for in a Mailing List Manager

The mailing list manager must, obviously, be able to accept the volume of data you want to manage. Examine any limitation on record size or number of records carefully. (A *record* is complete single entry.) Other things to keep in mind include:

- *Integration with list sources.* If you're buying names from an outside source, are these names available in electronic form? If so, can these new names be imported? How easy is this? (Please note that some list rental agreements only license the use of the list for one mailing, and do not constitute outright purchase.)
- *Merge and purge.* Related to the above, can lists be scanned easily for duplicates, and edited accordingly? This eliminates wasted postage, and prevents recipients from becoming irritated when they receive the fourth and fifth copy of your latest mailer.
- *Sample selection.* In many cases you'll want to do a test mailing. Does the software allow you to select a sample based on various criteria?

For example, one way of selecting a random sample is by selecting every "nth" record (10th, 100th, or whatever is appropriate to get the sample size you need.) However, you may want a *stratified* sample, one that reflects the weightings of various subgroupings in your list. Can you do this with the software?

- *Statistics/analysis.* What summary list statistics does the software produce (for example, counts by geographic territory)? Does it allow you to input the results of the mailing, in order to analyze which segments of the list produced the highest levels of results?
- *User-defined fields.* Does the software enable you to attach new fields? For example, you might want to include a list of your company's products or services that the customer has purchased.
- *Sort and screen flexibility.* A client with whom I spoke recently wanted to suppress mailings to an area of Florida that had been recently devastated by a hurricane. His software (mainframe-based, alas) did not enable him to do this. This is one of the advantages of a PC-based system, and the software should be able to exploit it.

   Conversely, you'll want to be able to target particular messages to particular segments of the mailing list. This is known as *database marketing*. The ability to easily "slice and dice" the data is very important for this reason.

   The ability to sort by zip code can actually save money on mailings, since the post office charges less for mail that is pre-sorted.
- *Marking.* Related to the ability to sort and screen flexibly, does the software allow you to mark or tag records individually for some later action? This is an essential feature if your list is going to work like you do. For example, you may want to send a follow-up letter to ten clients whom you saw last week at a trade show. Such an ad hoc list would have to be generated by marking each individual to be included.
- *Campaign management.* It is often important to be able to record a history of what has been mailed to each name on the list. This is especially true where there is a sequenced campaign of

letters (as there typically is, for example, when a magazine subscription is about to expire).

Profile of One Mailing List Manager—MarketPlace Business

MarketPlace Business is an infoware product ideal for business-to-business marketing. It contains a mailing list manager along with actual data—the names of 7 million U.S. businesses, as compiled by Dun & Bradstreet. It requires a CD-ROM reader and is very easy to use.

In addition to listing the name and address of each company, MarketPlace lists:

- The type of business by SIC (Standard Industrial Classification) code
- Type of site (headquarters/branch/single site)
- Annual sales
- Number of employees
- Type of ownership (public/private)
- Geographical area by state, county, metropolitan area, and zip code
- Year established
- Name and phone number for a contact individual

The program comes with an internal metering system that allows you to pay for only the names you use. You can immediately use 3,000 names when you purchase the software. You purchase the rights to use more names by calling the manufacturer and getting a password that unlocks the appropriate number of names contained in the CD-ROM's database. The manufacturer updates the list continually and issues a new CD-ROM every three months.

The program includes many sophisticated list management features, including:

- List counts
- Summary list statistics
- Random sampling
- List sorting

Mailing List Managers

- Export to other software packages
- Predifined report formats

A similar program for mailings to individuals was originally released along with the business-to-business file. It was withdrawn from the market after a number of right-to-privacy groups objected.

Major Mailing List Managers

	DOS	Windows	Macintosh
Professional Mail Arc Tangent, Inc. 21 Gray Avenue Santa Barbara, CA 93120-2009 (800) 350-8054	●		
AccuZip6 Software Publishers Inc. 16531 Bolsa Chica Street Suite 306 Huntington Beach, CA 92649-3595 (800) 233-0555			●
MarketPlace Business MarketPlace Information Corp. 3 University Office Park Waltham, MA 02154 (800) 999-9497		●	●

Lists on Disc

It is now possible to get mailing lists themselves in electronic form. This is handy for importing data into a list management software package. One of the most complete of these comes from American Business Lists, a Division of American Business Information. The lists they sell on CD-ROM disc include:

- 9.3 million U.S. businesses
- 1.6 million Canadian businesses
- 1.3 million high-income Americans
- 78 million consumers

The lists are also available in hard-copy labels, 3×5 cards, PC diskettes, nine-track computer tape, or through online access. The information on the business lists includes:

- Name of the owner or manager
- Business name
- SIC code
- Street address
- City, state, and zip
- Phone and fax numbers
- Number of employees

American Business Lists
5711 South 86th Circle
PO Box 27347
Omaha, NE 68127
(402) 331-7169

Chapter Five

Desktop Publishing

Desktop publishing is another category of software that most of us are familiar with. It's one of the first kinds of programs that drew the interest of marketing people. Advances continue to be made in this category.

Basic Description of Desktop Publishing Software

Desktop publishing (DTP) software has transformed the art of page makeup. It enables typesetting and page layout to be done on an inexpensive personal computer. This saves most companies substantial amounts of money previously spent on outside vendors for design, typesetting, and layout services.

DTP also improves the final product, in many cases. It enables changes to be made more easily and quickly, and invites an interactive approach to graphic design. Rather than being stuck with what you have, you can preview the results electronically and make adjustments accordingly.

Type can be set, graphics added, and recurring formats can be saved for re-use. The more sophisticated programs allow for advanced typesetting features like *kerning*. Kerning is the pairing of letters that look better linked than separated. The combination *fi,* for example is often printed without the dot over the *i.*

Another advanced feature is color separation, instructions that allow for multiple-color printing. What we think of as full-color printing actually involves four, separate, single-color runs through the press. It is important that each single color run lines up with the others, and that the colors neither bleed onto each other nor have white spaces between them. Output of documents in color from a personal computer has recently become more feasible with the advent of color printer technology (costing less than $1,000).

More sophisticated DTP software programs also allow output to a typesetting machine such as a Linotronic. These machines are available at service bureaus, which usually charge by the page. The advantage to using a typesetting machine is that they offer significantly higher resolution (as measured in dots per inch) than a desktop printer. The net result is that the print looks smoother, and somewhat more professional. The cost may be high, though. I was recently quoted $8 per page for Linotronic output of a 300-page document, which in that case was prohibitive. Very specialized (and expensive) equipment is also available that allows oversize output, so you can create posters and even billboards. Some service bureaus are beginning to acquire this equipment.

The latest in DTP is work-group DTP, which runs on a network. This allows up to 200 people to work on the editorial and page layout aspects of a given document. While most of these packages are designed for magazine and newspaper publishers, they could also be used for complex marketing documents, such as elaborate business proposals.

DTP is not just for do-it-yourselfers. *Time* magazine recently converted its layout to DTP software run on a Macintosh computer, and other major publications seem to being doing the same.

Professional-strength DTP software is, in fact, quite complicated to master for anyone other than a page layout artist. Amateurs have generally found advanced DTP software so daunting that a new generation of DTP software has recently been introduced for the rest of us.

Clip art is available for many of these programs. Clip art libraries are collections of graphic images (digitized pictures) that can be electronically "clipped" and imported into other applications. Clip art libraries are available for sale separately, although clip art comes bundled with some DTP software. ClickArt from T/Maker Co. (1350 Villa St., Mountain View, CA 94041; (415) 962-0195) is an example of a clip art library compatible with Macintosh, DOS, and Windows environments.

The digital formats for clip art images have been standardized around some common standards with names like TIFF, EPS, and PICT. These images will work with other kinds of software, like presentation software.

You can also bring in custom images with a *scanner*. Scanners range from printer-size machines to hand-held devices. Using the right software, you can use a scanner to pick up an image from a drawing or another document. (Please be sure to respect the source's copyrights.)

Kodak now has a system called Photo CD that will enable ordinary cameras to create digital images that can be stored on a compact disk. Up to twenty rolls of film, hundreds of photos, can be stored on one disk. If your computer is equipped with a CD-ROM reader (they all will be before long), you can crop and expand these photos, combine them with other graphics, and bring them into your ad or proposal.

In the past few years, high-end word processing programs have incorporated features formerly only found in DTP software. Creating multiple columns, newspaper-style, used to require DTP—now many word processors can do this easily.

Benefits of Desktop Publishing

Several factors argue in favor of desktop publishing over manual layout:

- *Cost.* In most cases it is less expensive to use DTP than to do pasteup manually. This is true in both high-volume situations, where salaried pasteup people can use DTP more quickly and efficiently than razor blades and rubber cement, or in low-volume situations, where once a system is set up, a relative novice can be used instead of expensive free-lance talent to create professional looking results. The costs of hardware, software, maintenance, and training must of course be factored into any break-even calculation.
- *Quality.* DTP can raise the quality of printed output considerably. This is especially true in a marketing environment where low-volume documents (business proposals, for example) play a key role in getting new business.

    Projects for which full typesetting wouldn't be cost effective can qualify for DTP treatment. DTP-generated documents can provide a competitive advantage in the marketplace over those produced on a word processor.
- *Greater control.* You have greater control over the final product using DTP. Creating the document becomes an interactive process, with chances for feedback and course corrections be-

fore the final output is produced. (This can slow you down sometimes, too.)

It's also possible to use DTP output to reduce the margin of potential error when the document is sent out for final printing. For example, copy can be sent containing actual crop marks, rather than simply measurements indicating where the cropping should be.

- *Organizational learning.* DTP allows design expertise to be stored in the form of *templates,* literally design molds into which graphics and text can be poured. Templates for various kinds of documents come bundled with the major DTP packages, and there is an active third-party market to provide others. This minimizes the need to reinvent the wheel. It may also bring about greater consistency in the marketplace, for example in a company with many offices that independently produce marketing materials. It also enables you to leverage the efforts of talented graphic designers, whose template designs can be used as the foundation for a complete corporate graphic identity.

Marketing and Sales Applications for Desktop Publishing

The following are some of the marketing and sales-related applications of desktop publishing software:

- *Brochures.* Brochures and flyers, whether a simple C-fold, or an elaborate glossy brochure, can be laid out, critiqued, and revised before being printed. Because an electronically-generated brochure is easy to revise, the brochure is dynamic and can grow as your business grows.
- *Proposals.* Likewise, business proposals can get very elaborate when large-ticket sales are involved. DTP is especially a boon in these situations, which are often nonrecurring sales. The ability to turn out a typeset proposal quickly can make the difference in a six-figure sale.
- *Ads and mailers.* Print ads and direct-mail pieces can be laid out. It is relatively easy to produce a series of messages that have a common core theme and design, with some variation.

There is even a program (Multi-Ad Creator from Multi-Ad Services, Inc., 1720 W. Detweiller Drive, Peoria, IL 61615, (800) 447-1950) that is optimized for producing one-page ads.
- *Catalogs.* Product and service catalogs can be prepared once, then updated for changes.
- *Customer newsletters.* There are few businesses today, particularly in the area of services, where creating lasting relationships is not a core element of the marketing program. A client or customer newsletter can do this, and give the customer valuable information at the same time. DTP gives such newsletters a professional look, with minimal cost and effort. Clients are more likely to read them, and to associate the company with professionalism and quality.

Case Study—Sales Training

One of the most innovative uses of desktop publishing also involved several other kinds of software.[1] After a large merger of two pharmaceuticals companies to form Smith Kline Beecham, Inc., training of the combined sales force was needed in several areas:

- The sales reporting system
- The national accounts strategy
- Sales resources
- Compensation and career opportunities

A software consulting house was hired to develop the training program. They used PC games as the model for the training materials. First they designed the screens on paper. Then, using an ingenious combination of desktop publishing, a word processor, and a drawing program, a series of illustrative storyboards was created. Finally, these were integrated and animated using another piece of software called a *scripting language* that integrated the files in the proper sequence.

The result was an interactive program that allowed the sales force to learn while having fun. The idea was so popular that it was exported to the company's regional sales office. One game, for example, taught employees about the company's products. As each question is successfully answered, the trainee is awarded one brick. The goal is to accumulate enough bricks to build a pyramid. (We note that at this writing the same effect might be achieved more easily by using multimedia authoring software—see Chapter 20.)

What to Look for in Desktop Publishing Software

Some things to consider when selecting a DTP package include the following:

- *Compatibility.* Does it work well with your word processor and any graphics software you're using?
- Ease of use. If you'll be using the program yourself, how difficult is it to perform basic tasks? How difficult is the program to master?
- *Advanced features.* Does it do color separations? Kerning? Can you achieve text effects, like rotating text? Does it contain a spelling checker?

Profile of One Desktop Publishing Package— PageMaker

PageMaker was the first commercially available desktop publishing program, and is still a leader in the field. Text can be input from most major word processing programs, or directly in PageMaker. This enables you to separate the intellectual functions of writing and editing from the aesthetic functions of page layout and typesetting.

PageMaker imports most graphics formats, including both those from clip art libraries and scanned images, such as photographs or original artwork.

Page layout features include headlines, page borders, and columns.

Typesetting features include complete control over font type, style, size, and direction on the page. An automatic kerning table is included for commonly found combinations of letters, and manual kerning can also be done.

PageMaker also has editing features, which include search and replace and a spelling checker. These features are similar to those found in most word processing programs.

There is a *control palette,* a tool-bar-like feature that enables rapid access to the most commonly used commands. Complete control over color is included, including linkages to no less than eight color matching systems (including Pantone). You can open multiple publications at one time, which makes it easy to lift material from one to another.

PageMaker runs under both Macintosh and PC/Windows environments, and the features and operation of both programs are virtually identical. More importantly, the documents you create under one environment can be transferred completely into the other environment. This translation feature includes text, graphics, and font specifications.

Major Desktop Publishing Packages

	DOS	Windows	Macintosh
PageMaker **Aldus Corporation** **411 First Avenue South** **Seattle, WA 98104** **(800) 333-2538**		●	●
FrameMaker **Frame Technology Corporation** **1010 Rincon Circle** **San Jose, CA 95131** **(800) 843-7263**		●	●
Quark XPress **Quark, Inc.** **1800 Grant Street** **Denver, CO 80203** **(800) 788-7835**		●	●

Endnote

1. Karen D. Moser, "Company Creates PC Games for Sales Training," *PC Week,* January 28, 1991: 59–61.

Chapter Six

Fax

There is no doubt that the age of the fax is upon us. These days most of the business cards I collect have both a phone and a fax number on them. When they were first introduced, faxes were a shared resource—a business or branch had one or two, located centrally. As models costing less than $1,000 became more prevalent, there was a tendency for each department to own one, then each cluster of offices.

Basic Description of Fax Software

Now fax has moved onto the desktop. With a *fax modem*, fax software can be used to fax documents directly from the desktop, and to receive incoming faxes. A fax modem can be an electronic card that goes inside the computer, or an external box that plugs into the computer. Fax software is used to send and receive faxes over the fax modem. It is analogous to communications software that drives a regular data modem.

Fax software simply changes the electronic document you want to send (a word-processed letter, for example) into an analog (non-digital) signal that can be sent over the telephone lines. You can then, of course, file your own copy of the document electronically. You do not first have to create a paper copy on your printer. This is more convenient, and spares the world's trees.

One of the disadvantages of this technology compared with electronic mail is that a fax image, once received, cannot be edited. To the computer it is simply a graphic block, like a picture. This has created a market for *character recognition* software, which translates incoming faxes into editable data that can be read into a word processor, spreadsheet, or other software.

Benefits of Fax Software

Compared to having a stand-alone fax machine, a fax modem is:

- *Less expensive.* Fax modems, particularly internal ones that fit inside your PC, are less than half the price of fax machines.
- *More convenient.* Faxing documents created in a PC application is literally as easy as printing them. There's no need to print a hard copy then insert that copy into your fax machine. This saves labor and the cost of paper.

I've found the quality of faxes sent directly from a PC to be equal to, or slightly better than, those sent from a fax machine.

The big disadvantage, of course, if that with a fax board you can't directly send documents that originated outside of your PC (a magazine article, for instance). Related to that is the fact that your outbound correspondence won't contain external graphics, such as the letterhead on your stationery.

In both cases, however, the document or letterhead can first be digitized using a scanner, then can be sent from a fax modem.

Marketing and Sales Applications for Fax

Some people think of fax as the universal electronic mail. Like e-mail, it is *asynchronous.* Both parties communicate sequentially—unlike with the telephone, where both parties can talk at the same time. Also, like e-mail, fax is fast—the transmissions move at the speed of light. Fax has the advantage that a much wider number of people have the hardware required to receive the message (i.e., a fax machine), where a computer is needed for e-mail.

There are various ways fax technology can be used in a marketing context:

- *Direct marketing.* Some of the marketing applications for fax technology are similar to those for direct mail. Fax can be used for mass "mailings" to a large list of recipients. This is known as *broadcast fax.* The computer keeps track of the database of names and fax numbers that the core message is being sent to. There are even list brokers who sell lists of fax numbers.

Fax messages can be sent to customers and dealers very quickly and inexpensively. There is no postage, and the time and expense of printing labels and stuffing envelopes is avoided.

Fax can create a sense of urgency to the communication. You can also precisely control the date and time of receipt of the message.

With fax, though, you can't control the physical quality of the output. Bear in mind that your gorgeous typeset-quality document may be coming out at the recipient's end on greasy thermal paper that must be cut into letter-size pages, and curls into a roll if left unattended.

Not everyone who receives "direct mail" faxes is enthusiastic about them. Some in fact see them as a pernicious electronic variety of junk mail. At this writing, administrative rules pursuant to the Telephone Consumer Protection Act of 1991 have been introduced by the Federal Communications Commission that would eliminate or at least limit this form of marketing.

- *Direct response.* Using a technology called *fax-back* you can selectively disseminate information of either a marketing or more technical nature. Fax-back, also known as *fax-on-demand* or interactive fax, is essentially a hybrid of voice response technology and outbound fax. Your customer or prospect calls in wanting information on a particular subject, let's say product specifications or a price list.

  Callers are guided through a sequence of choices they answer by using a touch-tone phone ("Press 1 for product information, 2 for price information," and so on). When all the choices have been made, each person requesting the information enters a fax number. The information is immediately faxed to that number.

  All of this occurs without intervention from an operator, which can save money. There is an obvious downside to this as well, as there is no chance for human interaction.

- *Surveys.* This is a cutting edge application for fax, and one that has a lot of potential. A colleague of mine recently needed to gather data quickly for an upcoming speech. He faxed out questionnaires, and had responses coming in later that day. This kind of turnaround is not possible with a mail survey. In addition, fax creates a sense of urgency in the respondent and an aura of timeliness about the information.

A recent technical development may break the fax survey area wide open. A software package called Teleform enables someone conducting a survey to fax a questionnaire to a list of potential respondents. The respondents then indicate their answers and fax back the answers. (So far, nothing new.) The software then electronically reads the incoming fax and converts it into database or spreadsheet information. All that is left for the user to do is analyze and interpret the results—the entire data-entry cycle is avoided.

- *Sales orders.* Teleform can also be used to directly enter incoming sales orders into other software. This procedure is known as *electronic data interchange* (EDI) (see Chapter 22).

Case Study—Telemarketing Follow-Up

Many successful telemarketing calls result in the person requesting that more information be sent. If this information is being faxed, the salesperson's time is then spent preparing the fax and sometimes in waiting in line to send it.

Exposition Excellence, Inc., a trade show planning company in Norwalk, CT, found that this follow-up could take over 10 minutes per call with a stand-alone fax machine—over an hour per day for each salesperson. After switching to a LAN-based fax server, the salesperson was able to send the information to the prospect without leaving his or her work station. This cut down considerably on the time for follow-up on each sales call. The net result was a substantial increase in the number of calls each salesperson was able to make in a day, and a subsequent increase in sales.

Later, broadcast fax was used to notify 500 clients of upcoming events. These broadcasts were unattended, and were set up to occur over a weekend when there was no other traffic on the system. (The recipients also probably thought this more considerate than sending it at peak incoming hours.)[1]

Fax   51

What to Look for in Fax Software

Fax software is generally tied to a particular fax board hardware design, and the two are sold as a package. The following purchase criteria refer to the hardware-software combination:

- *Ease of use.* Some fax programs require you to exit the program that created the document you want to transmit. In other cases you can do this from within the source application, which is much easier. In the latter case sending a document as a fax is done similarly to—and just as easily as—sending the document to a printer.
- *Compatibility with other software.* If you need to work with data created by other programs, can this be done? For example, how easy is it to use your existing contact list for a broadcast fax to all of the people on the list?
- *Network compatibility.* Companies or departments whose work stations are connected by a local area network (LAN) can use a single *fax server* package to serve everyone on the LAN.
- *Handling of graphics.* Some fax modems are better than others at sending graphics at a high level of quality.
- Enveloping. This is a handy—sometimes essential—feature that enables you to send multiple documents as part of one fax transmission.
- *Integrated OCR.* This capability is just beginning to be introduced. Incoming faxes are received as graphics, not text. You can't edit them with your word processor, or do much of anything else with them. There is now optical character recognition (OCR) software—the same as is used with a scanner—to convert these into editable files. Now this capability can be integrated into the fax reception, so the translation is automatic and no additional step is needed.

Profile of One Fax Package—Fax Manager

Fax Manager is a complete fax management system that works with many fax modems. It provides its own phone number management system. You can store frequently called phone numbers in "phone book" files. It allows group faxing, so you can send the message to a list of recipients.

Fax Manager provides a full range of information about a fax transmission as it is being sent, although it works in the background, so you don't have to interrupt what you're doing to use it. It can create an on-screen confirmation as soon as a fax is successfully sent. It also creates a log file, which tells you over time what was sent to what numbers.

You can also program a fax to be sent at a later time. This is handy if you want, for example, to send a long transmission at 3:00 in the morning, in order to avoid tying up your client's machine, and to save on phone charges.

One of the most amazing things about this software is that it can send a fax from within another application. For example, let's say you've finished drafting a letter you want to send to a client. You can send the document to the fax modem as easily as sending it to the printer. You can electronically attach a cover page to the document as a transmittal letter.

The newest version, Fax Manager Plus, has built in OCR, so that you can have incoming faxes translated into editable files. This can be handy if you need to incorporate the material into another document later.

Major Fax Management Software

	DOS	Windows	Macintosh
Fax Manager STF Technologies PO Box 81 Concordia, MO 64020 (816) 463-7972			●
WinFax Pro Delrina Technology, Inc. 6830 Via de Oro, Suite 240 San Jose, CA 95119 (800) 268-6082		●	
TeleForm for Windows Cardiff Software, Inc. 531 Stevens Avenue, Building B Solana Beach, CA 92075 (800) 659-8755		●	

Fax Back Systems

FlashFax
Brooktrout Technology, Inc.
144 Gould Street
Needham, MA 02194
(617) 449-4100

Endnote

1. Stephanie LaPolla, "EZ-Fax Lets Firm's Salespeople Do More Selling," *PC Week,* June 1, 1992: 91, 97.

Chapter Seven

Voice Mail

Many larger companies have voice mail systems that work through their PBX phone systems. If that's your situation, the technology described in this chapter will be redundant for you.

Basic Description of Voice Mail Software

Voice mail represents the union between two essential office technologies—the phone and the computer. In the past few years, voice mail has swept through corporate America like the personal computer did before it. Now the two technologies have been united in voice mail systems that run on a PC. These systems handle one phone line at a time.

There are more sophisticated PC-based systems that can handle up to 32 phone lines at a time. These however, are quite complicated to set up, and require a qualified consultant to do so. There are even larger systems that handle hundreds of phone lines at a time, but these more sophisticated packages require a minicomputer or even a mainframe to operate.

Voice mail software for the PC, like other communications software, requires additional hardware to operate. Specifically, it requires a special modem that is set up to handle voice signals. Like a regular modem, this voice modem may be in the form of a small external box that plugs into the computer, or it may be a board that plugs into the circuits inside the computer.

The software basically takes an analog signal—in this case a message—and digitizes it. It does this by *sampling* or measuring the signal at a high rate of speed. This is similar to the way music is recorded on a compact disc.

The fidelity of the signal is directly related to the sampling rate—the higher the sampling rate, the better the signal. Sampling rates of over 44 kilohertz—44,000 times per second—are common.

The resulting measurements are all, like any digital data, expressed in ones and zeroes. It takes a lot of ones and zeroes to represent a sound, even a single voice speaking. As a result, voice mail applications are very demanding of disc space. One megabyte of space will record about five minutes' worth of messages.

These packages are very capable, though. They can be used to set up voice mailboxes for 300 or so users. This number far exceeds the number of people who would realistically use the same phone line to try to retrieve messages. Several advanced packages support several phone lines.

They can be used to easily retrieve messages from a remote touch-tone phone, and the outgoing messages can be changed with a call in. They automatically record the time of the call, and can be used to store messages for later reference.

They can be programmed to have sequenced menus, so that the caller can navigate through a wide range of choices. In response to each set of choices, there is a voice message that the user has recorded in advance. (A touch-tone telephone serves as the microphone.)

Many packages have an *auto-attendant* feature. Used with a PBX system, this feature allows the system to direct the call to an extension specified by the caller, and to take a message if busy or transfer the call to an operator.

Another common feature called *forwarding* allows the machine to record an incoming message, then dial you at a new number you've specified, ask for you, wait for you to input your identification code, then play back the message. This way you'll reliably get messages quickly without having to let people know where you are. Some packages provide *background operation*, which means they can take messages while you're doing something else on the computer.

Having a voice mail package is like having a round-the-clock attendant who cheerfully and tirelessly conveys important information about your business. It's like a very sophisticated answering machine, but much more convenient to operate.

Benefits of Voice Mail

No business should allow phones to ring unattended, no matter what hour of the day or night. Human attendants—on staff, or working for outside answering services—are best, but expensive.

Compared to another low-cost alternative, a home answering machine, PC voice mail systems are:

- *Easier to use.* It's easier to perform basic functions like record outgoing messages and retrieve incoming messages.
- *Higher quality.* Because the messages are digitally recorded, they are generally of higher quality than those on answering machine microcassettes.
- *More flexible.* Most of the extended features listed in this chapter can't be duplicated by even the most sophisticated stand-alone machines.

Marketing and Sales Applications for Voice Mail

Voice mail is one of the mainstays of the telephone pornography industry. Now let's consider the more *legitimate* things that can be marketed using voice mail. There are two fundamentally different roles that this software can play—*inbound* and *outbound* telemarketing support.

Inbound telemarketing—where the consumer calls in—is often used in response to some other stimulus, like an advertisement on TV. Inbound telemarketing applications for voice include:

- *Conveying information.* The familiar "Press 1 for. . ." menu structure can be used to give the caller pertinent information on a self-selected range of topics. Many railroads give schedule information out this way, after you punch in where you're going, where you're departing from, and approximately when you'd like to depart.
- *Taking orders.* Callers can convey information both by using a touch-tone phone as an input device, and by leaving digital voice messages. Name and address, for example, can be left as voice messages, while product number and credit card number can be entered via the touch-tone keypad.

- *Surveys.* Callers can leave responses via touch-tone phone in response to prerecorded voice prompts ("Press 1 for yes, 2 for no, 3 for don't know.") Some voice mail software can tabulate the responses.
- *Sales force coordination.* One large consumer products company uses a large-scale voice mail system to coordinate the activities of its sales force. Meetings are announced, progress toward goals is reported, new promotions are described, and so on.

Outbound telemarketing voice applications—where the seller calls out—are high on most people's list of least-liked marketing techniques. The most familiar example, unfortunately, is the fabulous real estate offer in Florida.

There is nothing inherently wrong with the medium, however. It can be used to deliver a standard message to a predefined list of people. You can, for example, call your 250 best customers to let them know about a special sale to which only they are invited. The voice mail makes all the calls in sequence and automatically plays back the message. When it gets a busy signal, it tries again later.

The Telephone Consumer Protection Act of 1991 may influence the use of outbound telemarketing. As of this writing, the Federal Communications Commission has introduced rules to effectively ban electronic outbound telemarketing. These rules are being actively opposed by small businesses, who feel they have the most to gain from using this technique. The issue is likely to end up in court.

In any case, these new rules do not prohibit the use of outbound computer messages for polling, political messages, and solicitations by nonprofit groups.

Case Study—Company President

The president of a computer dealer (Personal Computers Plus, Hampton, NH) had been dissatisfied with call answering services.[1] He set up a Watson 1200 voice mail board to screen his calls as they came in. Each of a small number of high-priority clients was given a unique identifying number. When one of those clients called in, she or he was acknowledged by name with a prerecorded voice response. Then the call was put through to the president's phone. Other less urgent calls were recorded for a later response.

This created a way to screen important calls in real time, like a human operator could do at much greater cost.[1] The executive was able to make call-backs at a time convenient to him, while preserving the special handling needed for priority clients.

What To Look for in Voice Mail Software

Voice mail is a less competitive class of application than others described in this book. As a result, there is less copying of features, and more variations among the packages. You'll want to consider the following:

- *Ease of set-up.* Voice mail packages vary in how easy they are to program with hierarchical menus.
- *Compatibility with other equipment.* If you require a voice program to operate with your office PBX system, be sure the two are compatible.
- *Ability to shortcut voice prompts.* There are some systems that require you to listen to the full prompt before entering your touch-tone response. This can be annoying, especially if you call the line frequently.
- *Ability to drop to a live operator.* If you have an operator available, make sure your voice mail users can get to him or her. There are some interactions that it is best for a human to handle (an angry customer, for example.)

Profile of One Voice Mail Package—BigmOuth

BigmOuth, a popular single-line voice mail system, is a hardware-software combination—the software comes with its own PC circuit board. To use it, you have to take the top off your PC, remove a couple of screws, and plug in the board. Although easy for the experienced PC user, it can be intimidating if you've never done it before. If you have access to a PC support staff, they can help you with it. Otherwise, the manufacturer's support technicians will give you help by telephone if you need it.

BigmOuth has all the features mentioned above. It holds 300 mailboxes, and the number of messages is limited only by available disk space. It comes ready to use as a single-user system out of the box, complete with messages. It's easy to replace these messages with your own voice if you prefer. The screen gives you lots of information about each call, including the time it started and its duration. It's easy to review and delete or file messages.

BigmOuth can also be configured as a true telemarketing assistant, though this is more complicated. A prototype menu system is included to demonstrate BigmOuth's capabilities, and to guide the user in setting up a custom system. The system's enormous flexibility is somewhat offset by the difficulty of setting up, say, a menued answering system. Again, set-up is best left to the PC support types.

If you get a voice mail system, be ready to give it lots of disk space—my twenty-second greeting alone consumes over 65,000 characters of digital information. At this rate, a 360K floppy disk would hold about two minutes' worth of messages, and a 20 megabyte hard drive would hold a little over an hour and a half. Though this isn't a lot of recording time, it's enough if you maintain the system regularly.

One big drawback of any single-line system like BigmOuth is that when one caller is using the system, each additional caller gets a busy signal. Talking Technologies also markets a multi-line system called Voice Solution.

I leave BigmOuth on 24 hours a day when I'm not in my office at home. Now *that's* what I call getting your PC to work for you.

Major Voice Mail Packages

	DOS	Windows	Macintosh
BigmOuth **Talking Technology, Inc.** 1125 Atlantic Avenue Alameda, CA 94501 (800) 947-4884	●		
The Complete Answering Machine **The Complete PC, Inc.** 1983 Concourse Drive San Jose, CA 95131 (800) 982-3186	●	●	

Endnote

1. Kelley Damore, "Voice-Mail Cards Ease Distribution of Information," *PC Week,* October 8, 1990: 120.

Chapter Eight

Time Managers

For many of us, time is money, quite literally. Here are some tools to help us get a handle on this most precious nonrenewable resource.

Basic Description of Time Management Software

One of the basic themes in this book is that a personal computer is at best like a personal assistant—one that works constantly, quietly, and efficiently, and with very little management. Nowhere is this better exemplified than by the area of time management software. This is software that helps you schedule your day, then reminds you when things need to be done.

Sometimes this kind of software is referred to as a *personal information manager,* though that term has been used to mean so many different things that it has lost much of its meaning.

Time management software is basically a dynamic personal calendar. It lets you schedule meetings, deadlines, phone conferences, and personal events such as important birthdays. It can be used to schedule recurring appointments for each week or month.

It lets you assign the priority of an item, so if there is a conflict you know which one to attend to first. It lets you tag items as "to do" items, with reminders that keep appearing until the item is marked as completed.

Some of these same features are built into *electronic organizers* such as the Sharp Wizard. These are wallet-sized electronic devices that allow you to perform any of a number of functions, depending on the software card you have installed at the time. Some very busy people I know swear by these things. (So far, on the road I prefer a manual organizer. If I lose it—which I've done—I'm only out $20 or so.)

Benefits of Time Management Software

Woody Allen once said, "The key to success is showing up." He was only partly kidding. It's been documented that in business, and particularly in sales, persistence pays. It is hard to reach the clients and prospects you want to reach, yet you often can't or don't want to leave messages for them to call you back. You have to keep trying, and it often takes a half dozen calls before you connect.

Another thing we all agree it's good to do is manage relationships. *Relationship marketing* (there's another buzzword) is a fancy way of saying that if you build real bridges to people, they're more likely to *remember* you when they're ready to buy, and to *stay* with you after they buy.

On both counts, time management software is invaluable. It reminds you to follow up, even six months later.

Marketing and Sales Applications for Time Management Software

The applications of time management software in marketing are analogous to what they are in other areas:

- *Scheduling.* Scheduling of meetings, sales calls, and phone calls all are made easier and more flexible with time managers.
- *Follow-up.* Remembering to recontact people, especially if they've asked you to, is important in building and sustaining a relationship.
- *Project management.* Keeping track of several projects can be made easier.

Studies have shown that many sales are made after the fourth or fifth phone call or visit. But unless you're blessed with an extraordinary memory, it is difficult to remember to follow up with calls that need to be made, literature that needs to be sent out, personal visits, and so on.

One way to schedule such follow-up is with a hard-copy day planner (like Day-Timer, DayRunner, or Franklin.) Time management software works like these, with the following important differences:

- The software actually reminds you when something needs to be done.
- The software makes it easier to keep being reminded of things that still haven't been taken care of.

Many of the software planners create outputs that are compatible with the major hard-copy planners. The advantages of the hard-copy planners, of course, are that you can take them anywhere, and they are easy to use and inexpensive.

Note that some contact management programs, discussed at length in the next chapter, have some follow-up capabilities built into them. However, these features are not as well-developed in contact managers as they are in stand-alone time managers.

Clearly, the applications of time managers extend far beyond just marketing and sales. A busy executive in any function can benefit from this kind of software.

What to Look for in Time Management Software

Here are some things to keep in mind when selecting a time management package:

- *Integration with hard-copy systems.* If you're already using one of the commercially available hard-copy planners, does this software create printouts that are compatible with it?
- *Alarm.* Does the program have an alarm that alerts you to a scheduled event even if you're using another program at the time?
- *Flexibility.* Is the program easy to put information into and get back out? How easy is it to move a "to do" item that went past its original due date, and to assign it a new due date?

Profile of One Time Management Package—DayMaker

DayMaker for the Macintosh is a leader in time management software. It is relatively easy to enter events, thanks to full use of the graphic interface. It allows you to tag events as "to do," then reminds you, even weeks or months later, whenever you want to be reminded.

If you're doing something else with your computer at the time of the reminder, it comes on over whatever you're working on. If you're not using your computer at the designated time, the software "remembers" to remind you, and does so the next time you turn on your computer.

DayMaker is basically a highly structured database. As with any good structured database, it provides various views of the data:

- *The list view.* This is a complete listing of all information in the file.
- *The to-do view.* This is a list of only those items that are tagged as to-dos. The list is divided into a section for those items that have been done, and those that remain to be done. An item can be designated as done by dragging it from one list to the other.
- *The month view.* All events for one month. This defaults to the current month, but it is easy to switch between months.
- *The week view.* As above, for one week. This allows you to display more information about each event than the month view.
- *The day view.* As above, for one day. This contains the fullest amount of detail of any of the views.

The software allows a wide range of options for programming recurring events, including options like "The third Wednesday in each month." You can set the first and last dates at which the recurring events will appear.

Users can share DayMaker information across a network, so that groups can compare schedules for upcoming meetings. DayMaker even updates portable computers that have been detached from the network.

Each item can be tagged with a category, so that for example, the "to do" items on a particular project can be viewed at once. Each item may also be assigned a priority designation (high, medium, or low), and items can be viewed by their level of priority. This makes it possible to do simple project management with this software.

Any of the information can be viewed in Gantt chart format, that is, with a bar drawn horizontally between its start and ending dates. If you're using the software to schedule all of your activities, this feature can be useful in identifying times that are particularly busy or free.

The alarm feature, which is on at all times, can be customized to be either intrusive or subtle. You can set the alarm to remind you of an event

Time Managers

some preset time before the event occurs. There is also a snooze alarm feature that easily enables you to tell the software to remind you again in any length of time you specify.

DayMaker can be used as an "electronic Rolodex," to hold the names and addresses of key contacts. It can be used to dial a phone automatically. (I keep all phone numbers in a contact management program, the subject of the next chapter.)

Major Time Management Packages

	DOS	Windows	Macintosh
DayMaker **Pastel Development Corporation** **113 Spring Street** **New York, NY 10012** **(212) 941-7500**			●
On Time **Campbell Services Inc.** **21700 Northwestern Highway** **Suite 1070** **Southfield, MI 48075** **(800) 345-6747**	●	●	

Chapter Nine

Contact Managers

Basic Description of Contact Management Software

Contact management software is database software that has been specifically designed for keeping track of contacts. It is the electronic equivalent of a manual Rolodex or business card file, except that you can keep more information with it, and it keeps itself in better order. There is space for several *fields* or pieces of information—name, title, company, mailing address, phone and fax numbers, and other pertinent information.

There are often *user-defined fields*, you can keep track of information that is particularly important to your selling situation. If you're selling investments, for example, you'll want to know the level of risk tolerance in each of your contacts. This way you can bring to their attention those opportunities that best fit their stated preferences.

There are usually other fields that can be used for notes, that is, unstructured information about a contact. *Unstructured* information is information that varies among contacts. For one contact, you might enter the name of her administrative assistant in the notes field. For another, you may enter his home phone and fax numbers. Both structured and unstructured information can be searched and sorted at a later time.

Many of these programs contain built-in phone dialers and word processing software, so they in effect can operate as a command center for sales. They can also be used to send faxes directly, provided you have a fax modem.

Corporate CEOs and salespeople were the first to recognize the power of contact management software. There are now over 50 packages on the market, many of which offer similar contact and scheduling features.

Benefits of Contact Management Software

Contact management software represents a single solution to one of the biggest problems in marketing and sales: keeping track of customers and prospects, and maintaining a sustained level of contact with them. It provides one place to keep everything about a given account, including all of the contact people, orders they've put it, and details of phone conversations and meetings.

Dedicated software—software designed for contact management—is usually the best way to keep track of names, addresses, and phone numbers of contacts. Although this can be done with a generic database management program (see Chapter 18), these are generally slower and more cumbersome than contact managers. They also require much more time and expertise to set up.

Marketing and Sales Applications for Contact Managers

Contact managers are among a new breed of software that specifically addresses the needs of sales and marketing professionals. Sustained tactical and strategic contact with clients and customers is often the difference between wins and losses.

Levels of contact should be strategically programmed. For example, you may want to keep a low level of contact with a large list of prospects through direct mail and/or fax. You may want a higher level of contact with past clients and hot prospects, perhaps a periodic phone call. And you'll want a more intensive level of contact with current clients, including frequent phone contact and personal visits.

Contact management software enables you to keep logs of all types of contacts made with an account, and to plan upcoming contacts. They are also great time-savers, in that you can automatically enter appropriate contact information into a user-modifiable letter or fax cover sheet template.

Case Study—Account Management

Farmland Industries, Inc. is an agricultural supplies distributor. Its sales team sells fertilizer, feed, petroleum, and agricultural chemicals to 2,500 farming cooperatives throughout the Midwest.[1] They were having a farming cooperatives throughout the Midwest.[1] They were having a problem with "cross-selling" different products into their accounts. Although a co-op would need more than one of the distributor's products, a salesperson wouldn't always know that. More than one salesperson would often call on the same account without being able to determine the total status of that account.

Farmland wanted to turn their salespeople into *consultants* able to comprehend and respond to the total needs of their accounts. Most of their field salespeople were already equipped with laptop computers and modems. They built a LAN-based contact management system (using GoldMine software running under OS/2) that enabled salespeople to transmit their contacts to a central merged database. They found that this software enabled them to easily create customized data fields, including some for demographic information.

Farmland uses the scheduling feature to have salespeople record the time they spend with each client and to make comments about the visit. The system then generates weekly reports about each salesperson, which regional managers then use to evaluate the salesperson's performance. Among other things, they check to make sure they're spending appropriate amounts of time with the right accounts.[1]

This system allows Farmland's regional and corporate managers to check on the status of any account at any time.

What to Look for in a Contact Manager

There are several factors that vary significantly among contact management packages:

- *Speed.* You'll want to be able to retrieve information about a contact efficiently, quickly, and with few keystrokes or mouse clicks. How quickly this happens is a function of both the software and the computer you're running it on. Some packages run unacceptably slowly on slower computers.
- *Ease of integration.* If you're moving from another kind of mailing list, or if you'll want to export the data once you get your contact manager running, explore how easy it is to get information in and out of the database.

If you want to pool contacts with other users, can this be done, and how easily? Can sharing be done between IBM compatible and Macintosh users?
- *Flexibility of queries.* Be sure that the data you'll want to sort on can be used in that way. Some of these programs are surprisingly choosy about what they let you do with your data.
- *Template flexibility.* Be sure the program allows you to define a document as a *template,* that is, a prototype document you'll use many times.

Profile of One Contact Management Package—ACT!

ACT! is currently the best selling contact manager software, and runs in all three major personal computing environments (DOS, Windows, and Macintosh). The Windows and Macintosh versions operate virtually identically, and can share the same files. The DOS version runs on a network, which at this writing the other two versions do not.

ACT! enables you to manage massive amounts of information about each contact. There are 54 data items you can capture for each person on your contact list, including 15 that can be totally defined by the user.

This program has many advanced features that distinguish it from other contact software:

- *Built-in pop-up fields.* In many data entry fields, double clicking on the name of the field brings up a list of options. You can then select the option you want to enter by double-clicking on that option. These pop-up lists include commonly used state abbreviations, zip codes, job titles, and country dialing codes. Any of the pop-up lists can be modified by the user.
- *A to-do list.* ACT! has a built-in scheduler, simpler than but not unlike the one found in DayMaker. It allows the user to program reminders of items related to different accounts—phone calls, meetings, and other to-do's.
- *User-definable macros.* ACT! has a built-in macro function, which works on a "watch me" basis. A macro is a string of commands that can be executed as if they were one command. You turn on the macro recorder, do the series of things you want the macro to do, then turn off the macro recorder. You

then give the macro a name, and can execute it any time literally at the push of a button.

One macro can be defined as the start-up macro, the first thing the computer will do after launching the software. One handy way to use this feature would be to automatically print a list of all "to do" items scheduled for the current day.

- *User-definable icons.* Customizable icons and buttons were pioneered by Microsoft in the latest versions of Word and Excel. Many of the functions of the software are available on an icon bar, without having to go through the menu structure. The user can modify these icons, taking out ones that are never used, adding ones for new macros. Essentially this means the software can be configured to work exactly as the user works, while the core database structure remains the same.
- *Group edits.* Groups of records are easy to create, and can be edited together. For example, if a company address changes, all the records for people at that company can be updated simultaneously.
- *Links to GeoQuery.* The data stored in ACT! can easily be exported to GeoQuery, a geographic database package (profiled in Chapter 11), for further analysis. This powerful combination can be an advantage when defining sales territories, and in setting up trips to the field.
- *User-defined fields.* It is very easy to set up and define new fields. Any field, including ones defined by the user, can become the basis for a sort or select operation.
- *Built-in reports.* There are various useful report templates that come with ACT!, and others can be defined by the user. For example, there is a History Summary Report that summarizes, for a period of time defined by the user, all attempted calls, completed calls, meetings held, and letters sent for a particular account or group of accounts.

Major Contact Management Packages

	DOS	Windows	Macintosh
ACT! Contact Software International 1840 Hutton Drive Carrollton, TX 75006 (214) 919-9500	●	●	●
CAT IV Chang Laboratories, Inc. 10228 North Stelling Road Cupertino, CA 95014 (408) 727-8096			●
Maximizer Richmond Technologies & Software 6400 Roberts Street , Suite 420 Burnaby, BC Canada V5G4C9 (800) 663-2030	●	●	

Endnote

1. Mary Mann, "Contact Managers Help Distributor Harvest More Sales," *PC Week,* June 8, 1992: 111, 115.

Chapter Ten

Sales Force Automation

Sales force automation (SFA) is a very broad class of software. Much of it is custom-designed, or at least custom installed by a *value-added reseller* (VAR). A VAR is basically a hybrid between a retailer and a consultant—they supply turnkey solutions to business problems.

SFA has recently been given a real push by the availability of low-cost, lightweight personal computers. The most advanced technologies in both the IBM and Macintosh worlds are now available in laptop and notebook configurations (the latter generally weighing less than seven pounds). "Sub-notebooks" weighing four pounds or less are starting to be introduced, and probably soon they will have the same power as their larger siblings.

Basic Description of Sales Force Automation Software

"Sales force automation" is something of a misnomer, since not even the most ambitious software developer anticipates replacing salespeople with machines. *Sales force support* software is a more accurate (albeit ungainly) term. These systems act as intelligent assistants to sales people in the field.

Sales force automation generally involves a customized combination of many of the functions described in other chapters in this book, wrapped up with a standard hardware platform and package of training and procedures. The standard hardware platform includes the designation of a standard field-worthy, portable computer, a central server of some kind (often a mainframe) to gather and collate data sent in from the field, and telecommunications hardware, software, and protocols to connect the two.

Benefits of Sales Force Automation

Some of the benefits that implementers of SFA claim are:

- *Greater productivity.* Many salespeople are having to work with more accounts than previously. SFA helps make this possible.
- *Greater effectiveness.* Higher close rates per 100 sales calls typically are experienced.

Marketing and Sales Applications for SFA Software

Sales force automation software is inherently integrated software—it performs many functions. Many of the functions offered in SFA systems are abbreviated versions of the same functions that can be found in stand-alone software. However, in many cases, it is precisely the combination of functions that causes the sales force to be more productive.

The Sales Automation Association recently surveyed its members to find out what sales-related functions their members are performing on personal computers. Their findings[1] were that members use this software as follows:

Application	Current Usage
Word processing	84%
Electronic mail	83
Call history	81
Contact management	80
Call reporting	79
Electronic reports	66
Spreadsheets	60
Territory management	57
Sales forecasting	55
Lead tracking	51
Proposal generation	50
Inquiry/order entry	48

Application	Current Usage
Sales/market analysis	47
Time management	47
Sales presentations	46
Expense reporting	45
Sales management	44
Graphics	43
Pricing	42
Market/business planning	41
Schedule management	37
Telemarketing	29
Marketing management	26
Market research	23
Product demos	23
Geographic mapping	22
Desktop publishing	20
Product management	13
Electronic catalogs	11
Hiring and training	8

We note that many of these are generic business functions (word processing and spreadsheets, for example) needed by managers and executives in many functions. They need to be customized somewhat to be used in the field, but fundamentally they are being used as general business tools for people on the road, not as sales tools.

Another interesting thing about this list is that many of the sales support functions listed occur while the salesperson is off-line from the customer. The computer, in effect, is being used to automate the paperwork that salespeople need to complete at the end of the day or between calls, such as call reporting and expense reporting. The computer in many of these applications is not being brought in as an integral part of the sales process.

This profile could change radically as hardware and software evolves. For example, it is highly probable that in the near future a CD-ROM drive will be available that is light and small enough to be a standard feature in an under-five-pound portable computer. If that were the case, interactive sales presentations—including interactive videos—could be created to take on the road. A development of this nature could substantially shift the role of the personal computer in sales. The percentages using computers for "electronic catalogs" and "product demos" could shift significantly.

Another new technology that could impact sales force automation in the future is *pen-based computing* (PBC). Pen-based systems use an electronic stylus to record information on a custom-designed computer touch screen. Menu-driven questions can be answered by simply checking the response. Order entry is one sales function that can be automated using pen technology. Pen-generated reports may also eventually replace the manual call reports that many sales reps fill in after each call and mail to some central processing facility.

Case Studies

Since sales force automation systems are so highly customized, it is instructive to look at the approaches taken by several pioneers in this area.

Hanes

Sara Lee's Hanes hosiery division first started automating sales functions in 1972.[2] The first application was an inventory reordering system. Computer punch cards packed in each box were pulled by retail store sales clerks and physically sent back by Hanes for processing.

During the 1980s the product became bar coded, so that reorders could be transmitted electronically to Hanes. Shortly thereafter an *electronic data interchange* (EDI) feature was added so that the major retail chains could transmit ordering information directly to Hanes' computer. Other modules to increase the productivity of sales personnel were added along the way.

The payoff has been impressive. The time salespeople spend managing inventory has been reduced by 40 percent. The time devoted to writing orders has been reduced by 45 percent. Sales per person have increased by 45 percent, and the company has gained 16 share points with virtually no increase in sales costs.

Gillette

Gillette has used SFA to solidify relations with major retail chains.[3] Beginning in 1988, it began using pen-based computers to gather information from chain outlets. Gillette's merchandisers gather information from chain stores, including:

- Prices
- Promotions
- Displays
- Out-of-stocks
- Shelf conditions
- Competitive actions

This information is fed daily into a central computer and used to generate weekly reports for use by chain store account managers. By knowing more about their channels' businesses, they can help become more like business partners or advisors.

Campbell Soups

In addition to soups, Campbell sells frozen meals (Swanson), spaghetti sauces (Prego), and bakery products (Pepperidge Farm).[4] Its sales force consists of 300 account reps, who call on chain supermarkets' headquarters, and 900 retail salespeople, who call on the supermarkets themselves. Ideally, information flows both ways—from the field to the account rep, for example, in the case of inventory shortages, and from the account rep to the field when, for example, a chain buyer has approved a new product for sale in his or her stores.

Before SFA, data from the field would take six to eight weeks to be incorporated into reports to management. Conversely, the account reps had no efficient, structured way to notify salespeople of new products and promotions authorized by the supermarket buyers.

Over a period of 15 months ending in early 1988, a system was developed that used a hand-held computer and menu-driven software. The system could be used to call over 100 reports from the mainframe. Management was able to get actionable information in one to two days.

However, several problems cropped up during the implementation of the first generation of the system:

However, several problems cropped up during the implementation of the first generation of the system:

- The system had difficulty tracking data when the customers' regions did not conform to Campbell's regions.
- The system offered so many reporting options that most users were overwhelmed.
- The system was based on proprietary hardware technology. One result was that the reports still had to be printed out and mailed to the sales staff.

In 1990 the system was upgraded to run on standard-architecture laptops. It has now become an essential part of the salespeople's way of doing business.

Upjohn

This pharmaceutical company has 1700 detail representatives, each of whom is assigned between 400 and 600 physicians.[5] A key challenge is managing that list of physicians, for example, tracking their various days off.

Upjohn began its SFA efforts in 1985. After interviewing 50 sales reps, the systems designers began designing the system. Unfortunately, they were wildly ambitious in terms of what could realistically be implemented within a reasonable amount of time. For example, the original system design called for a module that would show the detail rep the best driving route to the physician's office. While no one argues its usefulness, its practicality is at issue. It is an application that remains in the testing lab even today.

A reduced system was designed, which included electronic mail, a database, and some territory management components. The system was implemented on standard-architecture laptops, and has been rolled out successfully.

What to Expect

Sales force automation involves a major commitment of time and money—usually over a year to develop, and a cost averaging $7,000 per person. All constituencies ultimately served by the system should be involved in its design. These often include:

- Field sales
- Sales support
- Sales management
- Marketing
- Customer service

Experts recommend that a selected group of field salespeople be used to pilot the effort, with subsequent rollout to the rest of the field sales force and then to the other functions. The MIS department and/or an outside SFA vendor serve as the catalysts for the project.

Major Sales Force Automation Vendors

Data One
4530 River Drive
Moline, IL 61265
(309) 797-3873

CSC Index Group
Cambridge, MA
(617) 492-1500

Envoy Systems
Waltham, MA
(617) 890-1444

Marketing Information Systems
Waltham, MA
Evanston, IL (708) 491-3885

Endnotes

1. Wendy S. Close, "A Software Diet to Fatten Sales," *Sales & Marketing Management,* October 1992: 76–82.

2. Thayer C. Taylor, "How SFA Blunts Outside Threats," *Sales & Marketing Management,* July 1992: 105–107.

3. Thayer C. Taylor, "How SFA Blunts Outside Threats," 105–107.

4. Curt Schleier, "Case Studies Times Two: SFA That's M-m-m-Good and a Pharmaceutical Roll Out," *Sales & Marketing Management,* March 1992: 59–61.

5. Curt Schleier, "Case Studies Times Two," 61–65.

Chapter Eleven

Mapping Software

Some of us remember—and others have seen in movies and cartoons—the days when sales territories were laid out on giant bulletin boards with push-pins and string. Now this is all done electronically.

Basic Description of Mapping Software

Mapping software enables data to be graphically shown on a geographic map. The more sophisticated of these systems are technically known as *geographic information systems (GIS)*. The desktop versions becoming common today evolved from complex mainframe and minicomputer systems.

The underlying data is kept in a database, which is usually separate from the mapping software. Most mapping programs link to data kept in common database formats. The data is depicted on the map in terms of electronic "pushpins" or dots, in the case of point-oriented data like the location of a company. Area-related data, like the median household income in a zip code, is depicted as a shading pattern or a color.

Most of these programs can map data to zip codes. The more sophisticated programs can map data at even finer levels—for example, to physical boundaries, such as highways and bodies of water.

In terms of complexity and sophistication, there are three distinct levels of mapping software. These are, in ascending order of sophistication:

- *Thematic mapping.* Thematic mapping packages allow you to express data attributes on a map using techniques such as shades, dots and similar symbols, and color. Generally you can manipulate and query the underlying data, but not the map

directly. An example is per capita income by zip code expressed as different shadings on each zip code.
- *Street/data-based mapping.* Data-based mapping programs map attribute data to specific points on the map, such as streets. You can manipulate or query both the underlying data and the resulting map.
- *Desktop geographic information systems.* These include all of the features of the above two, plus a greater degree of cartographic accuracy and spatial analysis tools.

Benefits of Mapping Software

Desktop mapping software has many advantages over manual tools such as physical maps and pushpins:

- They make it easy to reconstruct the map if a change is made.
- They make storing and retrieving maps much easier.
- They allow data elements to be associated with mapped areas.
- They enable you to quickly generate presentation-quality maps.
- They enable you to easily perform "what if" queries.

Marketing and Sales Applications for Mapping Software

Mapping software can be used by marketers and salespeople in the following ways:

- *Sales territory management or realignment.* You can quickly tell whether account assignments are balanced to the number of salespeople. Different scenarios can be modeled easily.
- *Target marketing.* If you want to send a direct mail piece to all customers and prospects within a bounded area (a given radius, for example), this is easy to accomplish.
- *Site selection.* Determining the optimal location for a retail outlet is much easier with this kind of software.
- *Distribution planning.* Warehouses and other storage and distribution facilities can be optimally located relative to account destinations.

- *Media planning.* With an underlying database of media outlets, mapping software makes it easy to target distributions of press releases. The case study below presents an example of this.
- *Competitive analysis.* By mapping your competitors' outlets against your own, you can identify points of conflict and oversaturation. For example, any retail bank undergoing a merger should conduct this kind of analysis to identify branch redundancies.
- *Sales prospecting.* It's easy to locate target accounts that are within the same general location. This is helpful when you're planning a trip into the field.
- *Analyzing business and demographic data.* Business lists (if you're a business-to-business company) or demographic and census data (if you sell directly to consumers) can be analyzed in order to pinpoint areas likely to be most productive for prospecting.

Case Studies

Public Relations Management

The first example is not so much a case study as an illustration of a software application built around a GIS. A software developer has developed an ingenious vertical market application that illustrates how mapping software can be used. The company, Desktop Solutions, has created a data management program called Public Relations Manager for public relations agencies. Based on the 4th Dimension database for Macintosh computers, the package also includes the GeoQuery mapping software and a Gantt chart program. All three software packages are linked in a seamless unit.

The key is that actual data relevant to public relations agencies and corporate communications professionals is also available from the software publisher. You have the option of buying files of print, broadcast, and/or periodicals outlets.

This enables you to quickly locate and contact appropriate media outlets within, for example, the radius of a particular location. This would be invaluable, for example, in setting up a promotion for a new store opening.

Public Relations Manager
Desktop Solutions
4315 Valley Green Mall
Suite 191
Etters, PA 17319-0189
(717) 938-4270

Demonstration of Service Delivery Capabilities

Another example of how mapping software is being used comes from the health care field.[1] Blue Cross, a large health care provider, uses Atlas GIS in making sales presentations to large employers across the country.[1] The mapping software is used to map the location of employers, their employees, hospitals and physicians under contract with Blue Cross and competing health care organizations.

The purpose of this is to demonstrate service gaps, which Blue Cross then proposes to fill. This kind of demonstration is essential to convince employers to sign on. A similar analysis used to be done by outside consultants, at five times what it now costs. The company also cites the advantage that it allows them to maintain better control over the data than when they used an outside vendor to maintain it.

What to Look for in a Mapping Package

The different categories of mapping software vary significantly in cost and in the amount of experience it takes to use them proficiently. For this reason, it's important to know exactly what you're going to want the package to do for you.

- *Geographic specificity.* Some programs map to larger levels, but not to finer levels such as census tracts.
- *Integration with other programs.* It is important to be able to easily manipulate the data underlying the map. You may have to import data from a corporate mainframe, for example.
- *Ability to use existing data.* It is much easier and less expensive to use commercially available data than have to create it. Some programs, for example, read TIGER files (Topologically Integrated Geographic Encoding and Referencing). These are digital maps of street segments created by the U.S. Census Bureau for the 1990 census, and available on CD-ROM or tape.

Mapping Software 87

Profile of One Mapping Package—GeoQuery

GeoQuery is a relatively simple mapping program for the Macintosh. It is targeted at the salesperson, particularly for use on the go in the field.

The basic program package includes a U.S. map with state boundaries, interstate highways, five-digit zip codes, and major cities. At additional cost, "atlas files" are available for:

- State maps
- Regions
- U.S. highways and major state roads
- ADIs
- DMAs
- SMAs

The result is that you only need to buy what you're going to use.

GeoQuery maps data down to the five-digit zip code level—but not below. This is usually accurate to within 2.5 miles of the actual location. Although not as accurate as street address matching, it is much less expensive. And it is sufficient for many important business applications, such as:

- *Setting sales territories.* This can be done based on an analysis of the amount of potential opportunity in each area, not simply the geographical area.
- *Planning business travel.* The software can tell you, for example, how many of your clients are within 10 miles of a particular location.

The program directly can access data on an IBM mainframe or DEC VAX. It also seamlessly integrates with other software such as 4th Dimension, ACT!, and Data Desk.

The program is extremely easy to get up and running. I had drawn my first map—using live data from a consulting assignment I was working on—within about 15 minutes of opening the package.

GeoQuery allows you to map multiple data sets on the same map. You could, for example, view store locations against average household income by zip code. The data can consist of individual records, in which case the software can aggregate the data, or of data that is already aggregated by geographic region (such as census or demographic data).

You can query the underlying data by graphically manipulating the map created by the software. For example, let's say you want to know the total sales of all accounts located within 100 miles of a given city. All you do here is draw a circle—or any other shape—around the city and ask for a summary report. The software goes back from the map to the underlying database and calculates the answer.

Records selected in this way can also be exported to another program—for example, to a mailing list package for a targeted mailing.

Major Mapping Packages

	DOS	Windows	Macintosh
GeoQuery GeoQuery Corporation 387 Shuman Boulevard Suite 385E Naperville, IL 60563-8453 (708) 357-0535			●
Atlas Pro (street/data-based mapping) Strategic Mapping, Inc. 4030 Moorpark Avenue, Suite 250 San Jose, CA 95117 (408) 985-7400	●		●
Atlas*GIS (desktop GIS) Strategic Mapping, Inc. 4030 Moorpark Avenue, Suite 250 San Jose, CA 95117 (408) 985-7400	●		
Atlas Mapmaker (thematic mapping) Strategic Mapping, Inc. 4030 Moorpark Avenue, Suite 250 San Jose, CA 95117 (408) 985-7400		●	●

Endnote

1. Erica Schroeder, "Strategic Mapping Helps Blue Cross Manage Data," *PC Week,* August 19, 1991: 29.

Chapter Twelve

Electronic Mail

Electronic mail, or e-mail, is another category of software (like word processing add-ins) that seems to be dying off as a stand-alone, and is instead becoming incorporated as a feature in other applications. Discussions in this book of other applications that contain e-mail as a feature will include mention of their e-mail capabilities. These other applications include:

- Sales force managers
- Groupware
- Public databases

The comments in the balance of this chapter generally refer to both stand-alone e-mail systems and e-mail imbedded as a feature within other applications.

Basic Description of E-Mail

Electronic mail software lets you send an electronic note or letter to one or several individuals instantly. Most e-mail works on a *store and forward* basis. This means that the electronic letter, rather than being sent directly to the recipient's computer, is first sent to a central electronic mailbox, which is usually located on a mainframe computer. The recipient must then go into the mailbox to get the message.

Electronic mail services contain directories of their subscribers, so you can easily look up who is on the system. (There are also unlisted accounts.) International standards for communication among different e-mail systems (X.400 protocols) have been established, but are being implemented relatively slowly.

E-mail contrasts with fax or voice mail, where the message is directly delivered to the end user's computer. Within the computing community, fax has largely been seen as an alternative to e-mail—where intended recipients were on incompatible systems, or no systems at all.

It is ironic that two of the latest developments in fax—fax software that works on a PC, and OCR software that translates an incoming fax into editable text—make the fax more like e-mail. E-mail may yet come back, though probably in a different form.

Like an online database, to use e-mail you'll need:

- A modem
- Communications software (described below)
- A valid account with the e-mail vendor

You can tell the truly high tech business people by the ones who have *three* phone numbers on their business card: phone, fax, and e-mail. Some companies—mostly software companies like Microsoft and Borland International—are run almost exclusively on e-mail.

Most e-mail systems have these features:

- *User directories.* You can tell if another person is registered on the system and what their mail number is.
- *Message answering and forwarding.* You can automatically address an answer to a message you've received on the system, or forward it to another user.
- *Copying.* You can send multiple copies of your message to different people.
- *Group addressing.* You can send simultaneous mailings to a group of users.
- *Archiving.* You can store your incoming and outgoing messages for future reference, organize them, and retrieve them at some future time.
- *Security.* Identification codes and user passwords keep someone else from accessing your mail or charging your account.
- *Message scanning.* You need read only the topic lines of all your messages first, then select those messages which you want to read in full.

Electronic Mail

- *Off-line composition.* You can create a message before you connect to the system to send it, thereby reducing on-line charges.

A very exciting feature to look for in the future is an interface to a wireless transmission system. Several e-mail vendors have announced their intention to develop and implement this feature. This will mean that you can send e-mail—or any other electronic document—to anyone, anywhere, via radio signals. More importantly, you won't have to check in for mail; it will just arrive (like a fax does today). The technology to do this is here now, it just hasn't yet been fully implemented in a commercial form.

Another current trend is for e-mail to be incorporated into other applications, particularly online information services (see Chapter 16). Consumer services such as CompuServe and Prodigy offer e-mail to other subscribers as just one of their many online services.

Most groupware programs (see Chapter 13) also contain e-mail modules for communicating within an organization.

Benefits of E-Mail

The applications for e-mail are essentially the same as those for fax, direct (physical) mail, and voice mail. It contrasts with those means of communications in the following ways:

E-Mail Compared to Fax

E-mail's main advantages over fax are:

- It creates an editable, searchable file on the recipient's computer.
- It does not require paper and ink. It is therefore more convenient and less expensive in terms of natural resources. (This is also true, of course, of PC-based fax.)

Its main disadvantages are:

- The document you're e-mailing must originate in electronic form. This precludes the use of hard-copy items like articles, paper letters, and so on. (Yes, these could be scanned, but the host mainframe e-mail computers don't usually recognize graphic files.)

- Because fax is point-to-point rather than store-and-forward, you know when you've gotten a fax—it comes out of the machine, or your PC alerts you. It takes more of an effort to retrieve e-mail.

E-Mail Compared to Physical Mail

E-mail has several advantages over physical mail:

- It is faster.
- It is easy to "broadcast" messages to a list of recipients.
- It is easier to store and retrieve messages.

Its disadvantages include:

- It has a small user base, relative to the number of people with physical mailboxes.
- It does not create a legally-binding hard-copy document, nor is it convenient for longer documents.

E-Mail Compared to Voice Mail

E-mail has several advantages over voice mail:

- It can be stored and searched later. Voice-mail messages can be stored, but only at great expense in terms of hard-disk space. They can't be searched later.
- It's easier to sort incoming messages. Information scientists at MIT have developed a system called the Information Lens that allows e-mail to be sorted at the recipient's desk, for example, by subject and/or by sender. This kind of technology, generically called message filtering, will probably be incorporated into most e-mail systems before long.

E-mail's disadvantages over voice mail are:

- It has a smaller user base.
- The user needs a PC instead of just a touch-tone telephone.

Marketing and Sales Applications for E-Mail

E-mail is useful where several individuals need to contribute to a document of substantial size that must be then edited and/or formatted electronically. It is ideal, for example, where several geographically dispersed company experts must collaborate on a proposal or sales presentation.

E-mail would be an ideal vehicle for narrowcasting messages to specific clients, were it not for the frustrating lack of standards and interfacing capabilities. Although technical interchange specifications have been developed, e-mail vendors have been reluctant to concede the proprietary nature of their current transmission formats. The development of a truly universal e-mail system should, I believe, be a high priority in supporting the continued competitiveness of U.S. business.

Case Study—Newsletter Production

A collaborative newsletter is also an ideal application for e-mail. The idea for this book came from a monthly column called "The Marketing Machine" that I wrote for a newsletter called *The Marcus Report*, targeted at marketing people in professional services firms. When I'd complete each article, I'd send it to the newsletter's editor, Bruce Marcus, over MCI Mail. Though we both live in New York City, sending it this way was much less trouble and expense than it would have been to get a messenger to deliver hard copy.

Bruce would then incorporate my article into his newsletter, and send the whole package—again by e-mail—to his publisher, who at that time was based in Toronto. There the final editing was done. The whole thing could be turned around quickly, and finally could be imported into page layout software for the preparation of camera-ready copy.

What to Look for in an E-Mail System

In any e-mail system, the following are critical elements:

- *The user interface.* How easy is it to use? Can it be customized using "front end" software that automates and simplifies many functions?

- *Linkages with other systems.* If you need to communicate with other e-mail users on other systems, is there an easy way to do this? These so-called *gateways* are slowly becoming more common, thanks to the recent development of industry standards in this area.

What to Look for in a Telecommunications Package

Telecommunications software is necessary to tell your modem what to do. Your modem is necessary in order to translate the *digital* signals created by your computer into the *analog* signals used by the phone system. (Someday we'll have digital phone lines, and modems will no longer be necessary.)

You'll need a telecommunications package to use e-mail, electronic bulletin board systems (see Chapter 22), or online databases (see Chapter 16). Note that most consumer-oriented online services—America On-Line, CompuServe and Prodigy—require their own, customized telecommunications software.

Some of the features that distinguish telecommunications packages from one another are:

- *Ease of use.* The user interface and general ease of doing things can vary significantly.
- *Scripting.* Some packages contain fairly powerful languages for automating log-on sequences and system passwords. These can be great time-savers.
- *Learn mode.* Some packages that do have a scripting language require that the commands be programmed manually. Others have a learn mode, which in effect is a macro recorder that enables you to create a script simply by sequentially creating each step of the sequence.
- *Directories.* Most telecommunications programs allow you to create directories of frequently dialed numbers, but these are easier and more logical to use in some programs than others.

Electronic Mail 97

Profile of One E-Mail System—MCI Mail

MCI Mail
1150 17th Street NW
8th Floor
Washington, DC 20036
(800) 444-6245

MCI Mail is one of the oldest e-mail systems. It is a dedicated system—e-mail and related communications are its only functions. It has about 100,000 users around the world. It can also send to the more than 1.8 million telex numbers worldwide, can send to fax machines, and can be used to create hand-delivered hard-copy mail.

MCI Mail contains a direct linkage with Dow Jones News/Retrieval, a major database system for company and financial market news. It also allows you to send messages to users of InterNet, an extensive academic and research network whose original development was funded by the U.S. government.

There is no monthly minimum—only a low annual maintenance fee and a modest charge for each letter transmitted. In most U.S. cities you dial in through a local or toll-free number, so phone charges are negligible.

The MCI user interface is command-driven and very austere. You have to know what you're doing, and it helps to keep a reference manual handy. Fortunately, you can automate most of the log-on procedures, including passwords, with communications software like Procomm or Microphone.

To make things even easier for MCI Mail users, Lotus Development Corporation developed an interface for IBM compatibles called Lotus Express, now marketed by MCI. There is a similar program for Windows users called The Wire. These programs will assist the occasional user in finding her or his way around the somewhat cryptic menu structure of MCI Mail.

Major Communications Software Packages

Programs Specifically for Linking To MCI Mail

	DOS	Windows	Macintosh
Lotus Express Marketed by MCI Mail 1150 17th Street NW Washington, DC 20036 (800) 444-6245	●		
The Wire Swfte International 724 Yorkland Road, Suite 150 Hockessin, DE 19707 (800) 237-9383		●	

All-Purpose Communications Packages

	DOS	Windows	Macintosh
Procomm Datastorm Technologies PO Box 1471 Columbia, MO 65205 (314) 474-9468	●	●	
Microphone II Software Ventures Corp. 2907 Claremont Avenue Berkeley, CA 94705 (510) 644-3232		●	●

Chapter Thirteen

Groupware

The information revolution that we are living through has many ironies. Computer networking is certainly one of them. Ten years after computers became "personal," one of the most significant developments is technology that links them through networks. A recent study conducted by Nolan, Norton & Co.[1] showed that as many as 70 percent of personal computer users in the United States are connected to a network.

Networks come in all levels of complexity. There are entry-level local area networks (LANs) that help as few as four users work together, for example in a small business office or corporate department. There are enterprise networks that tie local networks together, and wide area networks (WANs) that tie enterprise networks together. Companies that employ over 50,000 people worldwide now have all of those people networked together. They can communicate more easily and work together more effectively.

The hardware for networking was around for a while before networking really caught on. The reason for this is the usual one in the hardware business—there was no compelling software that required the hardware.

A new category of software called *groupware*, or work group computing applications, has changed this. There is now a reason—soon it will be an imperative—to link to people in one's own company, to one's trading partners (suppliers and customers), and eventually to other constituencies (large shareholders, the business press, and the financial community, to name a few).

Basic Description of Groupware

Groupware is a name that covers a category of software that enables groups to work better. By definition, it works only on computers that are linked through an electronic network. Groupware is at this writing a rapidly evolving category of software. New applications are being conceived and developed as you read this. Core functions include:

- *Electronic mail.* All of the basic functions, including sorting and storage.
- *Calendaring.* Shared scheduling of meetings, notification of meetings, and distribution of minutes.
- *Information sharing.* Posting of messages, computer dialogues, document libraries, etc.
- *Conferencing.* Real-time interaction of several parties via computer (so, for example, several geographically dispersed users can edit a draft document together).
- *Work flow automation.* Paperwork that must go through several individuals and departments can be tracked through its "life-cycle," the routing can be automated, and document integrity can be assured.

At best, these functions are integrated into a seamless work environment. Some of the packages can be customized extensively, so they work the way you do.

It is possible that soon groupware will disappear as a separate category—because *all* software will enable you to work with other people on a network. Many stand-alone packages have already been issued in network-ready versions. The days of the stand-alone desktop computer may soon seen seem like a quaint anachronism.

Marketing and Sales Applications for Groupware

The opportunities for groupware in marketing and sales have just begun to be explored. Here are some of the applications currently in use:

- Customer service
- Press inquiry tracking
- Project management

- Quality management
- Sales force management
- Sales presentations
- Strategic planning
- Telemarketing

Users of Lotus Notes, profiled below, are encouraged to develop their own applications and license them to Lotus for resale. This should hasten the availability of real-world, field-tested applications in all areas. A similar strategy was very successfully used by Lotus during the mid-1980s to broaden support for its 1-2-3 spreadsheet software.

Many of the groupware applications to date are *intra-organizational*—company employees talk to each other, albeit more efficiently. For marketers and salespeople, the real excitement will come from *inter-organizational* applications, those that reach beyond the boundaries of the organization. Once clients and customers link with a company's knowledge base, the possibilities expand considerably. Product introduction and availability announcements, pricing information, promotions, and customer satisfaction surveys could all be implemented on an inter-organizational network.

The whole area of market research as we know it could be transformed. For example, feedback on products in field test phase could be gathered and analyzed virtually effortlessly and instantaneously.

Corporate communications could also be transformed. Anything that currently goes into customer newsletters could be put into such a system. Press releases could also be distributed this way.

Benefits of Groupware

Groupware makes communications among people easier and more efficient. It creates a unified environment that contains the benefits of all of its pieces—electronic mail, scheduling, and conferencing—and becomes a necessity for many of those who use it.

Groupware can be used to develop custom applications at a fraction of what they would cost if they were programmed from scratch.

Groupware often has the beneficial effect of blurring boundaries:

- *Organizational boundaries.* People in different groups "talk" to each other regularly about common problems and their solutions.
- *Hierarchical boundaries.* The organization flattens as top management converses more freely with junior executives.
- *Geographic boundaries.* When using these systems, it seems possible to be everywhere at once.

In short, groupware makes the dream of the *virtual office*—a seamless organizational unity without many of the barriers that come between us—a real possibility.

Groupware also serves as a form of *organizational memory*, a support for the individual memories of the people who make up the organization. Important documents can be archived, and are available at any time and place. This enables important files, customer lists, and other documents to be used as the organizational resources they are—rather then being stuffed into file cabinets, unavailable to anyone except the person who remembers they're there.

In some cases groupware applications are being used to replace hard-copy management reports. Not only does this save on paper and reduce other distribution costs, it makes it easier for managers to use the information. By using key-word search, they can immediately focus on those parts of the reports that apply to operations they oversee. It's also easier to spot variances from plan or other situations that demand attention.

Case Studies

Corporate Communications

A corporate communications officer at an international professional services firm that uses Lotus Notes told this story to me recently. An issue had come up in the press that demanded an immediate response from the chairman of the firm. There were technical and political aspects of the issue that required consultations with principals of the firm in several of its offices around the country.

The communications executive created a first draft of the response using the word processor module within Notes. This draft was simultaneously and immediately dispersed to the principals whose input was required. The item was tagged with a special alert that indicated an immediate response was requested.

The executives in these other offices were able to retrieve the draft, and append changes and comments—all without leaving the Notes environment. These marked-up drafts were sent back to the communications officer over Notes, and were compiled within the software.

A final conforming draft was prepared, and sent via Notes to the chairman of the firm for final approval. The approval came back within minutes, again over Notes, and the resulting final release was sent to the press. The release was ready to be transmitted to the press within a matter of hours after the need for a press response had been identified. Compare this with the days such a process would have taken previously.

The benefits went well beyond getting the job done with fewer hours expended, although there certainly were some savings there. More important was the ability to generate a rapid response to a breaking news story involving the company. As anyone who has been involved in a public relations crisis can testify, being able to mobilize quickly is essential to being able to manage the issue—far preferable to having to react to it.

Account Management

Continental Insurance uses Notes to keep track of complex risks, such as oil refineries and airlines.[2] Each account requires an elaborate set of procedures on a scheduled basis. These procedures include safety inspections, regulatory filings, and other reports—over 170 tasks altogether.

The system was developed by extensively customizing Notes so that the forms and procedures would stay the same as they had been. But all of the generation, transmission, and storage of the paperwork is now done electronically.

A similar system could have been built from scratch. Indeed, a couple of years ago it would *have* to have been. But by using Notes as a foundation, the system was developed in one-third the time, and at less than half the cost, of a custom system.

What to Look for in Groupware

Groupware is a complex buy, one that often includes purchasing hundreds of identical packages at once. Some of the significant differences among the major packages are:

- *Feature mix.* Groupware is a somewhat flexible term, and as yet it has no consistent definition. As a result, the features vary from package to package. For example, Lotus Notes, the leading package in the category, does not include a scheduling module.
- *Integration with hardware.* Groupware varies as to the hardware requirements of the machines it runs on.
- *Integration with other software.* If you need to build bridges to other software your company is using, you'll want to check how well the packages work together.

Profile of One Groupware Package—Lotus Notes

Lotus Notes is one of the oldest groupware applications, and has smoothly integrated many of the various features of this class of software. Notes is now being used by over 120,000 users at over 400 companies. It requires an OS/2 server, and users must have Windows. An ordinary DOS machine cannot use Notes—nor can such a machine use any of the major groupware products. As of this writing, support for Macintosh users has been announced, but it's not clear when this will be available.

Notes is basically a database environment, in which reside various applications in the form of templates. The result is that Notes is very flexible, and can be customized to work like the company already does. It contains a sophisticated e-mail function that includes address books, message encryption (for security purposes), and keyword search for retrieving documents. The mail feature can be used to send documents created by another program (a spreadsheet, for example).

Notes includes its own reasonably sophisticated word processing software. The only major work-group feature not supported by Notes is scheduling.

A number of third-party vendors support Notes with *vertical applications* developed for specific functions and/or industries. Lotus includes

50 sample applications along with the purchase of the program. These include tie-ins to real-time news feeds and sales support applications. These sample applications can be used as is or modified. One add-in (Lotus Notes Document Imaging), for example, allows a Notes user to store paper documents such as faxes and letters in electronic form, then view them with Notes.

Lotus has a very active program to support these third-party developers. Their intention is to help establish Notes as the *de facto* industry groupware standard. A similar strategy, by the way, earlier helped 1-2-3 become the spreadsheet standard.

Lotus Development once predicted that Notes would eventually provide more of its revenue than 1-2-3. While this is far from happening now, Notes is so far the most promising application in this important growth area.

Major Groupware Packages

	DOS	Windows	Macintosh
Notes **Lotus Development Corporation** **5 Cambridge Parkway** **Cambridge, MA 02142** **(800) 343-5414**		●	
Windows for Workgroups **Microsoft Corporation** **1 Microsoft Way** **Redmond, WA 98052-6399** **(206) 882-8080**		●	

Endnotes

1. Mark Moore, "Survey Finds End-User Computing is Growing," *PC Week,* November 2, 1992: 151.

2. John R. Wilke, "Getting Together," *The Wall Street Journal,* April 6, 1992: R8.

Chapter Fourteen

Presentation Software

The function of many of the tools we've discussed until now is to get you in the door—to get you the appointment that will enable you to directly convince the decision maker to buy your product or service. Sooner or later though, it all comes down to personal selling. A professional sales presentation can make a good impression and set you up to close the deal. Presentation software can help make your presentations first-rate with minimal expense and effort.

Basic Description of Presentation Software

Presentation software creates presentations—those impressive-looking documents that go sideways on the page. (In computer parlance, they are in *landscape mode*.) They usually contain graphics, bullet points, sub-points, and headlines for each slide. The form of output can be:

- Hard copy
- Overhead transparencies
- 35 millimeter slides
- A "slide show" that runs directly on the computer.

If you're running directly from the computer, you'll of course need one when you give your presentation. You'll also need *one* of the following:

- *A large CRT screen.* It must be large enough for all of your viewers to see clearly.

107

- *A CRT projector.* This works like a projection TV, and can usually be rented from a provider of audio-visual equipment for conventions and trade shows.
- *An LCD transparency projector.* This is a device that plugs into the output from the computer, and has a transparent screen about page size (8 1/2 × 11"). The images generated by the computer are fed into the LCD screen, which in turn sits on top of a regular overhead transparency projector. The resulting images can then be viewed like overheads.

When running from the computer, you can advance slides either by clicking a key on the keyboard, or by using a pre-set timing pattern. This kind of setup can be ideal for a self-running slide presentation at a trade show.

There are some other advantages to running your slide show from the computer. For example, you can incorporate animated sequences and movies into the presentation. Unless you need such advance capabilities, however, it's probably better to stick with 35 mm slides or overheads as output. In general, they provide fewer opportunities for unpleasant surprises at speech time.

A deck of presentation slides is rarely a stand-alone document. It usually is accompanied by an oral narrative, and serves to emphasize points through visual reminders to the audience. As such, it should *support*, not compete with, the person talking. Hard copy—which can have one or several slides per page—can also be circulated as leave-behinds at the end of the meeting. Each person in the audience then has a tangible reminder of your points that they can refer to later.

Note that if you hand out the hard copies *before* you speak, you are likely to be drowned out by the shuffling of papers as your audience looks to what lies ahead. You also invite the kind of question that starts "On page 38 you say . . .", long before those points have entered the flow of your presentation.

The leaders in presentation software have outliners integrated with the slide program. You generally use the outliner to enter text, and the slide mode to enter graphics and format the presentation for output. You can switch back and forth easily between the two, and a change made in either slide or outline mode is instantly reflected in the other mode.

Presentation Software

Major changes in the presentation's overall structure—the order of slides, or the arrangements of points on a slide—are easy to effect. In outline mode, it's a matter of dragging highlighted text from one spot to another. In slide mode, there is a slide sorter that enables you to see several slides at once, and to drag slides around to change the order of the presentation.

Often some drawing and graphing tools are integrated into the software. While these generally are not as sophisticated as their stand-alone counterparts, they are convenient and nice to have when you're in a rush. You can also import charts, tables, graphics, and text that you've created within other applications.

Each slide has a master that enables you to set all formatting once and apply it to many slides. It becomes, in effect, a template that contains the look of the entire slide show. Colors can be set for all text, graphics, and backgrounds. Graphics can be applied universally to each slide in the show. For example, your company's logo can be scanned in and placed in a corner of each slide.

Presentation packages usually come with their own *clip art* (pre-packaged libraries of graphic images). They usually can incorporate commercial third-party clip art as well. They also come with background templates that can be used to rapidly format a slide show. You can also create your own slide show templates for later recall, so that all of your presentations have a consistent appearance.

Some presentation programs can incorporate multimedia features such as full-motion video. This enables you to, for example, click on a section of pie chart, and launch a movie that illustrates that segment.

Benefits of Presentation Software

For the purposes of preparing hard-copy output or overheads in black and white, a good word processor can be used to make a decent presentation. Of course, a word processor has no support for color, is often ill-equipped to work with graphics, and can't output to the CRT or color slides. Besides, good presentation software makes it easier to set up a professional-caliber presentation.

Presentation software makes it possible to generate impressive, persuasive graphics at a fraction of the cost of making 35 mm slides from scratch.

Marketing and Sales Applications for Presentation Software

The names of two of the leading presentation packages, PowerPoint and Persuasion, describe accurately the uses of these programs. They can help you make the *points* that *persuade* your prospect to buy. This can be useful in the following ways:

- *Delivering sales presentations.* These can be standardized presentations, or presentations customized to the needs of a particular prospect or group of prospects.
- *Giving speeches at trade shows and conventions.* The software can also be used to give a self-running demonstration or sales pitch.
- *Sales force communications.* Motivational speeches and other internal communications are enhanced with professional graphics.

What to Look for in Presentation Software

There are significant differences among presentation programs:

- *Ease of use.* Does it contain an outline feature? How easy is it to edit in the outliner and to move between slides and outline format?
- *Spelling checker.* Is one included? This can save some embarrassing moments while you're at the front of the room.
- *Graphics.* Does clip art come with the package? Is it the kind you need for what you're doing? If not, what other commercial graphics are available for the package? How easy is it to import and manipulate them?
- *Output.* Can you create the kind of output you'll need, for example, color slides?

Profile of One Presentation Package—PowerPoint

PowerPoint has been around for a couple of years, but has recently been revised to make it the premier presentation program. It has a combined outliner and slide program. Any changes—including font formatting—done in one mode show up instantly in the other.

PowerPoint has the new Toolbar feature that Microsoft is putting into many of its programs. This makes it easy to move around and execute commonly used commands.

Various formats for hard-copy output are available. You can create a notes form of output with the slide on half the page, leaving room to type in talking points related to the slide. You can also create an audience-handout format that has four, six, or eight slides on each page. It's easy to restructure the whole presentation by reordering the slides.

PowerPoint enables you to make 35 mm slides, provided you either have an *image recorder* or have access to one. An image recorder is a device (they generally cost over $5,000) that translates software files into exposed 35 mm film. The film can then be developed and processed as usual.

There are several service bureaus that have image recorders and that specialize in translating electronic output into finished slides. Genigraphics is one of these slide preparation houses.

PowerPoint comes with its own customized communications program, Graphics Link, that enables you to transmit files electronically (using a modem) to Genigraphics for output to an image recorder. Alternatively, you can send them a file on disk by mail or express delivery. Genigraphics processes the output very quickly, usually within 24 hours. The finished slides are expressed back to you.

PowerPoint has features that make your presentations sophisticated from a graphic point of view. It handles color very flexibly. Slide backgrounds can be shaded in gradations, a feature that makes them look professional.

PowerPoint comes in both Windows and Macintosh versions. The interface design and command structures are identical in the two versions, as are the file structures. This means that files can be easily shared by PowerPoint running on either of the two platforms.

PowerPoint contains drawing tools, including lines and geometric shapes, for spicing up presentations. All of the shapes, which include arrows, can be resized, rotated, stretched, and compressed.

Templates that include presentation formatting information can be prepared, saved, and used later to create similar-looking presentations.

This is helpful if you want your company to have a standard look for presentations. The program comes with 40 prefab templates for each of the four output formats the program supports: black and white overheads, color overheads, 35 mm slides, and on-screen presentations.

You can create *progressive disclosure*, or "build" slides that add bullet points one at a time as you speak. This can be a very effective way to highlight each point in a series, yet at the same time preserve the continuity of the list.

The program comes with its own spelling checker included and has a complete search-and-replace function. It contains a fairly complete set of graphing tools that enable you to created pie charts, bar charts, and the like without leaving the program. PowerPoint comes with a wide range of clip art drawings, including state and country maps, and business symbols. It also imports most commercial clip art libraries.

You can add full-motion video and sound to your presentation. The program also contains a run-time version, so that you can send a presentation on disk to someone else, and they can view it without owning the software themselves.

Major Presentation Packages

	DOS	Windows	Macintosh
PowerPoint Microsoft Corporation 1 Microsoft Way Redmond, WA 98052-6399 (206) 882-8080		●	●
Persuasion Aldus Corporation 411 First Avenue South Seattle, WA 98104-2871 (206) 622-5500		●	●

Chapter Fifteen

Spreadsheets

Spreadsheets are used by just about everyone. Most of their specialized applications are in the area of financial analysis. But they also have powerful applications in sales and marketing.

Basic Description of Spreadsheet Software

Spreadsheets are the software that need no introduction. They were among the first packages to achieve widespread commercial success, and are usually among the first software a computer user buys.

Spreadsheets are often taken for granted, and their capabilities under exploited. They basically contain calculational capabilities, database features, and the ability to create graphs easily from calculated data. (These three features were partly responsible for the name 1-2-3.) The database features are at best rudimentary when compared with a dedicated database program (see Chapter 18).

Each of the major spreadsheets contains a fairly complete programming language called a *macro language*. This enables sophisticated functions and complex keystroke sequences to be executed quickly and easily. It also enables sophisticated models of business processes to be constructed.

Macro languages have created a whole subindustry of third-party companies that develop applications to run under a spreadsheet. These applications are customized instructions for the spreadsheet that allow it to perform a particular specialized set of functions. There are, for example, advanced financial analysis routines for calculating things like the net present value and internal rate of return.

113

Benefits of Spreadsheet Software

Two true stories from my own consulting career will illustrate the benefits of spreadsheets. My first assignment as a junior consultant with a large consulting firm involved preparing cost and expense projections for a planned major addition to a hospital. In those pre-PC days (this was 1979), we used cream-colored oversize paper called spreadsheets. The largest of them had about two dozen columns.

We used calculators to figure each number, then wrote it into a cell on the spreadsheet. Correcting errors took lots of eraser rubber—unless they were so extensive that the whole thing had to be rewritten. The building of alternate scenarios, of course, had to be done from scratch on separate sheets. Our client paid for all of this labor—but that was just the way things were!

A year later I was engaged to build a mathematical model of New York State's sales tax revenue base. This involved a great deal of economic research to get data on actual sales in each of about 250 categories of products and services.

Today this basic research would still have to be done. But the part that came next seems archaic now. I hired a programmer to mount the model on a mainframe system that state budget analysts could refer to and "play with." This entailed several weeks of a programmer's time. The result, which was state-of-the-art at the time, was difficult to access and use by today's standards.

Electronic spreadsheets are such useful applications that in the early 1980s many sales of IBM-compatible machines were made to people who needed them to run spreadsheets, particularly Lotus 1-2-3.

Marketing and Sales Applications for Spreadsheets

Spreadsheets can be used in several productive ways in a marketing context:

- *Survey analysis.* Survey data in raw tabulation form, for example, is difficult for decision makers to understand and use. Putting key findings into a spreadsheet can allow you to look at them in a hands-on, dynamic way.

- *Data presentation.* Related to the above, the powerful graphics features of most spreadsheet programs can help you get your point across. The graphs can be electronically cut out and pasted into research reports and presentations.
- *Forecasting.* Market potential and sales trends can be forecast using spreadsheets. Most spreadsheets can be used for multiple linear regression analysis; others can fit data to curved trend lines of various descriptions.
- *Pricing.* Pricing for complex, customized products and services can be built up easily and quickly using a spreadsheet. For each consulting project I undertake, I first construct a spreadsheet that shows each task to be undertaken, the estimated time to complete it, and the hourly billing rate of an individual with a skill level appropriate to the task.

  Thanks to a template I've prepared in advance that contains formulas and formatting information, all of the extensions are performed instantly and a document worthy of presentation to a client is prepared.

  The best thing about this is that if during the proposal the client wants to change the scope of the proposal (that is, the amount of work), I can make such a change while I'm on the phone with the client. This preserves the momentum of the selling cycle.
- *Tracking new business.* I use another spreadsheet template that tracks business proposals outstanding. Each proposal, of course, is associated with a dollar value, but in addition I input an estimate of the likelihood (expressed as a percentage) the engagement will be commissioned by the client. Based on my most current discussions with the client, I revise these estimates every week. This gives me a running *expected value* for the work that I expect to book in the near future.
- *Profitability analysis.* Profits by product line and category can be analyzed on a historical basis, and can be forecast. "What-if" scenarios can be tested using different assumptions for pricing, market share, and overall market size.
- *Budgeting and planning.* Budgets often go through many iterations before being agreed to by all parties. Moreover, budgets

in the real world tend not to be zero-based, but rather to be incremental variations from the previous period. Both of these factors make them ideal applications for electronic spreadsheets.

Case Study—Price Quotation System

ComputerVision (formerly Prime Computer) is a computer maker and systems integrator. They offer 4,500 products in about 20 categories. Most sales include custom-configured hardware and software. It used to take salespeople an average of four days to put a price quote together.

Using Excel, they developed a price quote system that allowed this to be accomplished in fours hours instead of four days.[1] Development time for the system (about four months) was much shorter than it would have been if the system had been custom-coded from scratch.

Sales reps keep the system on their laptops, so they can generate simple quotes and custom proposals on the spot. The output quality is high, so that the quote the rep leaves behind is contained in a professional-looking document.

What to Look for in Spreadsheet Software

There are significant differences among spreadsheet programs:

- *Ease of use.* How easily can data be entered and manipulated? Is it easy to resize columns and rows?
- *Formatting.* If you're producing output for senior management or clients, how easy is it to produce professional-looking output?
- *Customizability.* Can the macro language be learned and programmed easily? Is there a *debugger* for spotting and correcting errors?
- *Capacity and speed.* Does the software hold enough data? When fully loaded, does it run acceptably fast on the hardware you're using?
- *Graphics.* Does it produce graphs of sufficient power and flexibility? How closely is the graph mode integrated with the spreadsheets mode?

- *Data access.* You may need to import data from other sources (for example, commercial online services, the company mainframe, or other PC programs). Can you do this easily?
- *Computations.* If you need a particular kind of non-standard computation, can the software accomplish this? If not, is there an add-in template that will do this?
- *Bulletproofing.* If the spreadsheet is going to be used by non-savvy users, can it be protected from inadvertent disruption?

Profile of One Spreadsheet Package—Microsoft Excel

Excel runs in both Macintosh and Windows versions, as do many Microsoft products. Files can be easily exchanged among the two formats.

At this point Excel is the leader in bringing new features to the spreadsheet market. It exploits the graphic user interface to enable the user to do things easily and quickly. For example, many commonly used functions are available at the click of a button through the Toolbar, which Microsoft is now implementing in many of its packages.

The program has some amazing intelligence features built in that can save the user time. If you start a series "January, February . . .", Excel guesses that the rest of the series is the names of the other ten months. (If it isn't, of course, you can change it by entering the correct data.)

It will do this same data-series extension with numbers, too. This makes it very easy to construct trend lines around actual data, then to extend those trend lines into the future. The ability to do this is at the heart of most forecasting models, and Excel makes it look easy.

Another time-saving feature is the way Excel guesses at data-parse formats. Data parsing means breaking down a continuous stream of data into discrete chunks. It's what you'll need to do if, for example, you download time series data from an online service like Dow Jones into a spreadsheet for further analysis.

Although most spreadsheets can parse data, Excel makes it easy. Excel scans the data and guesses how you'll want to have it go into the spreadsheet cells. Again, you have a manual override if the software's guess is wrong.

Excel contains a powerful macro language and many sophisticated functions. Since it is a popular package, there are lots of third-party add-ins written for it. Each macro does a very specific computation or formatting sequence.

One add-in is @ RISK (pronounced "at risk"), which runs on both Mac and IBM versions of Excel. There is also a version for Lotus 1-2-3. @ RISK provides Monte Carlo simulation, a sophisticated forecasting and modeling function. This would be useful, for example, in analyzing various scenarios for market share penetration for a new product. @ RISK is published by Palisade Corporation, 31 Decker Road, Penfield, NY, 14867, (800) 432-7475.

Spreadsheets can be linked, so that you can easily aggregate data. This can be very useful, for example, in aggregating sales data by region in order to arrive at total sales. It is also very useful for building up divisional budgets from those of smaller business units.

Major Spreadsheets

	DOS	Windows	Macintosh
1-2-3 Lotus Development Corporation 5 Cambridge Parkway Cambridge, MA 02142 (800) 343-5414	●	●	●
Excel Microsoft Corporation 1 Microsoft Way Redmond, WA 98052-6399 (206) 882-8080		●	●
Quattro Pro Borland International 10 Victor Square Scotts Valley, CA 95067 (408) 438-8400	●	●	

Endnote

1. Sara Humphry, "Excel Chosen for Speedy Development, Quality Output," *PC Week,* June 24, 1991: 144.

Chapter Sixteen

Online Databases

The term database is not very descriptive, in that depending on the context it means different things with only minimal relation to each other. In this chapter it is used to mean an online database system, usually running on a mainframe, that is called up over the phone lines.

That seems clear enough. The problems begin when we learn that each database *system* is made up of dozens or even hundreds of database *files*—and they're both loosely referred to as a database. Think of the database system as a department store, and the database file as a department within the store, and let's leave it that. (To add to the confusion, we'll see yet another use of the term "database" in Chapter 18.)

Basic Description of Online Databases

Using an online database is in some ways like using an e-mail system: you need a modem, communications software, and a valid user account and password. Each system has its own set of commands, and some of them are relatively difficult to use.

There are over 4,000 databases now available commercially. The database world has actually split into two distinct segments, each with its own set of audiences and applications in marketing. I'll call these segments *professional databases* and *consumer databases*.

To make matters even more confusing, there are also online services called *electronic bulletin boards*. To reduce the confusion, I've dealt with those in a separate chapter (Chapter 22).

Professional databases are what researchers use to retrieve information. They specialize in having huge amounts of information available for online searching, much of which appeared earlier in hard-copy form.

Having access to one of these systems is equivalent to having an electronic library at your fingertips. They cover trade and scientific journals, major magazines and newspapers, and directories.

Examples of professional databases are:

- Dialog
- Lexis/Nexis
- Dow Jones News/Retrieval

Professional databases tend to be priced on a pay-as-you-go basis, often with a very complicated and confusing list of charges and rates. The more you use, the more you pay. Charges can exceed $200 per hour, and you need formal training before you can effectively use these systems.

Consumer databases, on the other hand, are directed at consumers, and it is reasonable to think that one day they will be a potent force in marketing to consumers. They are already used for online shopping, whereby orders for consumer goods can be placed electronically. Consumer databases usually have an e-mail feature, which the professional databases do not.

Examples of consumer databases are:

- Prodigy
- CompuServe—which also contains many professional features
- America Online

Most consumer databases started life with pay-as-you-go price structures. Most have lately been moving toward flat-rate pricing, with a fixed charge per month giving the user unlimited usage of at least certain services. Often there are premium services, for which you pay a higher flat rate or a usage rate. This pricing structure has been bolstered by the advent of *advertiser supported* systems, pioneered by Prodigy. Other systems are *user supported* in the sense that their revenues are totally derived from user charges.

This subtle niching of the online market has happened over the past couple of years and will probably continue. We can expect there will be even more specialized electronic forums, as has happened during the past 20 years in other media like cable TV and magazines.

The only thing that might forestall such proliferation is if a single source is able to become a true online superstore and gradually pre-empt its competitors. The model for this is here already, in the sense that each of these databases has separate interest areas that the user can visit electronically. (Depending on the system, these are called *forums, files,* or *special interest groups.*)

Prodigy, by the way, achieved another significant innovation—its user interface. While the other programs were all command-driven and character-based, Prodigy was menu-driven and graphics-based. This means that it is easier for novices to use and looks more attractive.

The advances Prodigy has made come at the expense of some drawbacks. It is slower to use—but its flat-rate pricing structure has helped overcome the *economic* disincentive to use slow systems. Faster modems will eventually take care of the other major disincentive—the system's sluggishness.

The other disadvantage is that, because of its customized front end, it runs only on IBM-compatible systems. Most of the other systems listed here use generic communications software, and can be run on any machine that runs that software.

America OnLine recently mounted a significant challenge to Prodigy, and is now the fastest-growing consumer-oriented database system. Its proprietary front-end software has versions for Macintosh, DOS, and Windows.

Benefits of Online Systems

Imagine having all the world's largest business and general-interest libraries available at your fingertips. This, in effect, is what online database systems are. Each one holds a number (often hundreds) of database files—and each file in turn contains hundreds of publications. These are available for searching—by using a computer language specific to the database, you can retrieve on a PC the exact information you're looking for.

These searches can be done one time, or can be set up to be repeated at a frequency you specify. In the first case, suppose you're about to begin a market test of a new product. You might want to use an online database to locate the results of other tests of similar products. This can help you avoid mistakes that may have been made in the past, and to capitalize on the market successes of others.

In the second example, suppose you want to know about something a specific set of competitor companies does. You can set up a search that sweeps for all relevant information on, say, a daily or weekly basis. The result can be sent to you in hard copy or electronically transmitted to your PC.

Anything that can be done online can also be done manually. That is, you can send a person to the library to find the information in either case listed above. Doing this manually, however, is very time consuming and expensive.

The benefits, then, include the following:

- *Cost displacement.* It is often possible to use online information instead of doing original primary research, which costs substantially more.
- *Increased environmental awareness.* A focused program of information and retrieval can substantially increase a company's overall competitiveness.
- *Better targeted intelligence.* Online systems help in doing one's homework in a strategic situation. For example, if you're pitching a substantial piece of business to a company, you'll be better able to address their needs if you understand what's going on in the company. And you'll look a lot smarter!

Marketing and Sales Applications for Professional Databases

Professional database systems have several marketing and sales applications, mainly in the research area:

- *Getting background on companies, industries, or individuals.* When you're making a major pitch to a company you've never worked with, it's best to get some background information on the company and the individuals who will be making the decision whether to buy your product.
- *Competitive intelligence.* Competitors' advertising campaigns, product introductions, executives, and major client relationships can be tracked through trade journal articles.

Online Databases

- *Scoping markets.* Before doing original research, which is expensive and time-consuming, a quick check on an online database can yield valuable information on a particular market.
- *Identifying contacts.* Similarly, articles about a company, market, or product often introduce experts on the subject, whom you can then contact for further elaboration.
- *Generating target lists.* Databases usually contain lists of companies, such as those produced by Dun & Bradstreet. These can be sorted for specific criteria to generate custom mailing lists for business marketers.

There are several kinds of information available through online sources that are especially valuable to marketers:

- *Periodicals.* These include:
    - The general business press *(Business Week, Forbes, Fortune, The Wall Street Journal, New York Times)*
    - The trade press—both functional ones like *Advertising Age* and industry ones like *American Banker*
    - Regional newspapers—these can be a surprisingly rich source of information about companies and their activities
- *Newswires.* Examples are Dow Jones, Associated Press, Reuters, and Bloomberg News. Some of these are available as real-time feeds directly to a PC or to a dedicated terminal. Others are available only on an archived basis.
- *Broadcast transcripts.* Transcripts of significant radio and TV broadcasts, such as those by CNN and the BBC, are available.
- *Market research reports.* Individual products, product lines, or whole industries can be covered in these sources.
- *Investment reports.* Wall Street analysts pay close attention to market developments affecting the companies they cover. These analysts speak directly with the managements of these companies, and their reports can contain information not found elsewhere—for example, operating results by line of business.
- *Annual reports and 10-K filings.* These can be valuable in assessing the strategies of key customers, prospects, and competitors.

- *Executive biographies.* If you're making a pitch to an individual or group of individuals, it is important to know their backgrounds and learn how they think and act. A biographic analysis of the decision-makers can provide valuable insights.
- *Company listings.* These are valuable for identifying prospects and competitors. They can be searched by a variety of criteria (like industry, size, and location.) Listings of officers and directors are typically included.
- *Trademark registrations.* Both federal and state registrations are included. This can save a lot of time in determining whether a brand name is already in use.
- *Press releases.* Many companies routinely put their corporate communications out through wire services dedicated to this function (for example, *PR Newswire*). These can be important sources of information about product introductions and company strategies.
- *Census data.* Gross statistics are available on a census tract or zip code basis.

As is true of most online information, the amount of information varies by vendor, from full-text to prepared abstracts to simple headline citations.

In addition to being available through online systems, many of the sources are increasingly available through CD-ROM disks. Although these systems are not real-time, most of them update the information periodically by physically shipping a new disk. If this is sufficient, and if the same information is going to be used frequently, this may be a more cost-effective way to access the information than doing so online.

Marketing and Sales Applications for Consumer Databases

Consumer databases are being used by marketers in several ways:

- *Online shopping.* Many goods can be purchased online, and the order paid for with a credit card. Online catalogs will become more sophisticated as better graphics can be transmitted. There are also classified ad services available.

- *Online advertising.* Again, better graphics allow more attractive and informative advertising to be created. One major advantage over broadcasting is that advertisers are able to *measure* precisely the number of people who view their advertisements. Special promotions can also be supported this way.

  The infomercials that we see on late-night TV could really blossom online. During the recent presidential election, several of the candidates (including the successful ones) and their supporters used online services to communicate directly with voters.
- *Customer service.* After-sale product support is a key element of the sale, particularly with complex products like computer software. Many computer companies use online databases to disseminate information on new products, to answer questions about products, and so on.

  This approach could be applied to other industries as well. The owner of a new car, for example, may have lots of questions for the people who designed the car. While now it is virtually impossible to get this kind of interaction going, with electronic forums it could happen relatively easily.
- *Product distribution.* Software companies distribute updates and "fixes" to their software via online services. This is a specialized use that now applies only to information-based products but that could be used to supply the *information component* of any product.
- *Survey primary research.* Marketers are beginning to use online surveys to quickly get information that otherwise might be available from focus groups (see Case Study below).

Case Studies

Political Polling

During the 1992 Presidential campaign several of the candidates went online into electronic forums to answer questions from their constituencies. The power of this new medium in mass politics—one of the greatest marketing games around—was demonstrated for the first time. Clinton and Gore made the heaviest use of this medium—and, of course, won the election.

It was no coincidence that this occurred during the great PC price war of 1992—during which hardware prices fell by 10 percent per month at times, and the first truly capable machines priced under $1,000 were introduced. Many consumers were drawn in for this first time by these prices, as well as the wide availability of the machines and the software to run on them.

After the election, the new administration continued to test public reaction through online services. It became possible to instantly download all public presidential communications through several online services, and to likewise write to the White House.

Consumer Research

Nickelodeon, the children's cable TV channel, recently used online "focus groups" to get real-time reactions to its programming. Using a private forum in CompuServe, a nationwide panel of 75 children communicate regularly with Nickelodeon's research staff in New York City. They are used to test new programs via videocasette before the programs are aired. The only requirement for membership on the panel is ownership of both a VCR and a computer. Half the sample are minorities, and half are girls. Family incomes range from $20,000 to $120,000.[1]

Online focus groups eliminate travel costs and reduce to a few hours the time needed to get reactions to new programs or advertisements. It has been added to the network's formal set of research tools, along with more traditional research sources and techniques.

What to Look for in an Online Database

In choosing an online system, you'll want to think about:

- *Content.* You'll need to make sure that the sources you want to access are on that system. Some sources appear on several systems but in different forms.
- *Pricing.* Both pricing levels and the way the prices are structured (as described above) are important.
- *Ease of use.* Online systems can be complicated to master. Some offer "front-end" software (the CompuServe Information Manager, for example) to make things easier for the novice who has not yet committed all of the commands to memory.

Profile of One Professional System—Dialog

Dialog is one of the oldest database systems, having started life during the 1960s as an internal research system for Lockheed Aerospace. Dialog now contains nearly 400 databases, covering business and economics, science and technology, law, medicine, and current events. It is the single most complete database system for general business use.

Each database contains information gathered from dozens or even hundreds of periodicals. Much of the information is in the form of *abstracts,* that is, summaries of the original article prepared specifically for online use. The trend, though, is toward having *full-text* information available online, in other words the complete article as it appeared in the original journal.

There is a low annual fee to maintain an account on Dialog and no monthly charge or minimum. You are charged for the time you spend searching each database, plus the time to print the results. Search costs are set by each database producer (remember our department store analogy?) and vary from less than $30 per hour to more than $300 per hour.

While these costs may seem high, bear in mind that a huge volume of information can be searched in a fraction of the time it takes to manually search such materials (even if you own the physical source materials). A feature called OneSearch allows you to search up to 20 databases at the same time using the same search terms.

Searching is done by means of specialized Dialog commands that require some training and practice to become proficient at using. These commands are used to select the files and look for occurrences of *key words* that relate to what you're researching. The way that an electronic information search is designed is called a *search strategy.*

You may want to use several terms with *or* between them to indicate that the presence of one or the other term is sufficient. For example, in searching for articles describing trends in bankruptcy, you'll want to review articles that contain information on "bankruptcy" *or* "insolvency" *or* "Chapter 11" *or* "Chapter 7."

On the other hand, you may want to do an *and* search. This means that all the conditions you specify must be present. For example, if you're trying to locate a company in the Southwest that manufactures cotton garments, you'll want to use "Southwest" *and* "clothing" *and* "manufacturer."

Search strategies are much more complex than this, but that's the general idea. At any given point, you can tell how much information you've located before you print it out (and incur the print charges). The system keeps a running tab of your charges, and you get a final accounting at the end of each session. A skilled electronic searcher can usually get a lot of information in a $100-300 search.

Dialog has its own software for IBM compatibles called DialogLink. This speeds and simplifies searches. Macintosh users can use any communications software package.

Dialog is available 24 hours a day, except for Sunday mornings, when the system is maintained. There is a non-peak-hour service called Knowledge Index, which makes many of the Dialog files available at substantially lower prices.

There are many Dialog files of particular interest to marketers:

- *ABI/Inform (File 15)*. A comprehensive database for general business information. Contains input from over 800 primary publications.
- *PTS Promt (File 16)*. Another general business database containing abstracts and full-text records from more than 1,000 business publications of all kinds.
- *Trade & Industry Index (File 148)*. A database containing articles from over 1,500 trade journals.
- *PR Newswire (File 613)*. A database of the complete text of press releases issued by companies, PR agencies, trade associations, and government agencies.
- *Investext (File 545)*. A database of over 200,000 full-text reports written by investment analysts at 120 investment banks and research firms worldwide. Coverage includes 15,000 companies and over 50 industry groups worldwide.
- *PTS Newsletter Database (File 636)*. Full text of articles from over 400 newsletters in 40 industries.
- *Dun's Market Identifiers (File 516)*. A very complete business directory. Contains detailed information on nearly 7 million U.S. business establishments, both public and private. Includes address, product names, financial data, and marketing information.

Online Databases

There is increasing coverage of international business news available in the United States in English. Also, depending on your industry, there may also be specialized databases for that industry.

Profile of One Consumer System—CompuServe

CompuServe is a fee-supported, consumer-oriented system that began life as a computer hobbyists' bulletin board. It also contains some professional features. Under pressure from other flat-fee services, CompuServe recently moved to flat-fee pricing for basic services.

CompuServe includes many different kinds of services:

- *Electronic mail.* To and from other subscribers of the service.
- *Forums.* Also known as SIGs (Special Interest Groups). These cover a wide range of topics, including science and technology, computer hardware and software, and financial matters. Several major software publishers hold technical discussions here. The "PR and Marketing Forum," for example, contains discussions among marketing professionals.
- *News.* You can get news, sports, and weather directly from sources such as the Associated Press.
- *Travel and leisure.* The *Official Airline Guide* is available here, as is the SABRE airline reservations system.
- *The electronic mall.* Many kinds of products and services are available for purchase, including books, music, gourmet foods, health and beauty supplies, clothing, computers and other consumer electronics, office supplies, and discount securities brokerage services.
- *Financial information.* Market quotes, financial analysis, company information, earnings forecasts, and financial advice.
- *Entertainment and games.* You can play various games with other online opponents, and also get news about movies, music, and other entertainment fields.
- *Reference.* There are encyclopedias, government publications, census and other demographic data, and other reference sources.

There are several optional front-end packages, including the CompuServe Information Manager and The Navigator, for helping new users get around the menu structure. Software like this is available for both IBM compatibles and the Macintosh.

Major Online Database Systems

Unless otherwise noted, you may use any telecommunications software to access the database. See the end of Chapter 12 for a listing of such software. Your software package must, of course, be compatible with the computer you're using.

Dialog
Dialog Information Services, Inc.
3460 Hillview Avenue
Palo Alto, CA 94304
(800) 334-2564

Has IBM-only software for accessing at high modem speeds (9600 bps).

CompuServe
CompuServe, Inc.
5000 Arlington Center Boulevard
Columbus, OH 43220
(800) 848-8199

Dow Jones News/Retrieval
Dow Jones & Co., Inc.
PO Box 300
Princeton, NJ 08543-0300
(800) 522-3567

Nexis /Lexis
Mead Data Central, Inc.
PO Box 933
Dayton, OH 45401
(800) 227-4908

Can also be accessed through a proprietary data terminal.

Prodigy
Prodigy Services Co.
445 Hamilton Avenue
White Plains, NY 10601
(800) 776-3449

Must be used with its own IBM-compatible software.

Online Databases

America Online
America Online, Inc.
8619 Westwood Center Drive
Vienna, VA 22182-2285
(800) 827-6364

Must be used with its own front-end software, which runs in Macintosh, DOS, or Windows environments.

Endnote

1. "Nickelodeon Sets Up Online Focus Group," *The Wall Street Journal,* March 29, 1993: B1.

Chapter Seventeen

Survey Software

Personal computers are not only very good at computing, they're also good at compiling and communicating information. For this reason, they could in the not-too-distant future revolutionize the way market research is done. At this writing, though, market research is still an emerging application for the technology.

Most cross-tabulations are still done on mainframe computer systems, which provide limited flexibility and, being prohibitively expensive, require the use of an outside contractor. The time is ripe to migrate these applications to more flexible, user-friendly desktop platforms.

Basic Description of Survey Software

Survey software facilitates several steps in the research process:
- Survey design
- Data collection (known as Computer Assisted Telephone Interviewing, or CATI)
- Tabulation and data analysis

The most advanced software incorporates all three functions into an integrated environment. First, you design the survey using a built-in word processor. Then, presuming you're doing phone interviews, your interviewers can directly input the data into the computer as they're getting the answers. In more advanced systems, skip patterns can be programmed, such that the computer knows, for example, to skip Question 9 based on the respondent's answer to Question 8.

Finally, the data is analyzed for patterns and trends. Often such analysis starts with *cross-tabulation* of the data. This basically consists of first identifying the most significant *segments* of the population surveyed, then testing to see whether there are significant differences among them.

In consumer research, demographic breaks are most often used as the *banners,* that is, the segments being analyzed. Age, sex, family size, household income, and ethnic origin are categories commonly used to analyze data.

The answer to a particular question may also be analyzed based on the answers to another question. Suppose, for example, you're doing research that will be used on designing a new model car. You may want to cross-tabulate various attribute preferences to see how they relate to each other. You've decided that, given your target market, the car should have front wheel drive. You're sitting on a mountain of research data and must now recommend whether the car should also have air bags, and if so, how many.

You'll want to take a subset of answers from those people preferring front-wheel drive, and analyze the responses to another question on air bags.

In business-to-business research, company demographics are important. The size and industry of the company may provide valuable breakdowns, as may the title and/or functional area of the respondent.

A survey system can provide flexible tabulation schemes. If one breakdown doesn't yield significant differences, you can aggregate some of the categories, or try a new scheme altogether. Sure, this can be done when using an outside TabHouse, but in fact it rarely is, given the relentless nature of deadlines and budgets.

This brings us to a key benefit of personal computer survey systems—their *interactive* nature. Not only are they flexible, they allow an analyst to view the data in different ways until significant patterns emerge. One publisher of survey software refers to the "data sandbox" that every true analyst loves to play in, but often doesn't get to because we've given control of our data to an outside contractor.

There's another key advantage of survey software running on a PC. With a computerized survey there is no separate data entry step, as there traditionally is, because the interviewer directly inputs the answers at the time of the interview. This saves the time-consuming and error-prone step of transferring the data from another form (usually a paper survey)

Survey Software

to machine readable form. There is less elapsed time involved, less personnel time, and less chance for error.

It does, of course, require that the interviewers be able to type, and to be able to do so while they're talking.

To sum up, the results of using desktop survey software can be qualitatively *better*, and at the same time *less expensive* than the old way of doing things.

Marketing and Sales Applications for Survey Software

Research is an essential marketing activity. Its applications include:

- Designing future products
- Evaluating user reaction to new products
- Assessing competitor activity
- Testing pricing structures and price points
- Testing customer satisfaction
- Measuring employee awareness of products and promotions

The trend, as in many areas, is toward getting research information on a fast turnaround basis. Again, this argues for computerization of much of this activity.

Mail Surveys

We've concentrated in most of this chapter on telephone surveys because they are the most widely used type. Other forms of survey can also be enhanced or made more productive with information technologies. Surveys can now be both distributed and automatically tabulated using fax software. This software (TeleForm, described in Chapter 6) may someday replace the traditional mail survey. Faxed surveys have been recently shown to have higher response rates and shorter response times than mail surveys.

Focus Groups

Another productive form of research is the focus group. This is basically a semistructured group interview of between 6 and 12 people, led by a trained moderator. Focus groups have also been touched by new technology. *Audience response systems* enable a focus group moderator to get instant feedback from participants through wireless keypads. The

get instant feedback from participants through wireless keypads. The responses are instantly tabulated and displayed on a computer monitor in front of the group.

What to Look for in Survey Software

It's important to note that the packages we're discussing here are complete survey systems, not just questionnaire design packages. There *are* packages that assist with survey design, but in general the data must be exported from these in order to do much meaningful analysis.

Features to look for in a survey system include:

- *Integrated front end.* One of the objects here is to eliminate the translation step in between gathering the data and analyzing it. The system should have its own data collection module that interfaces seamlessly with the analysis module.
- *Interfaces with other programs.* If the package does not contain a data collection module, how easy is it to bring in data collected within another program? If the package does not include an integrated graphic output module for charting your results, how easy is it to output the results to another program that can do this?
- *Flexibility.* This includes the ability to tie together certain variables in order to define new aggregate variable categories; variable definitions of row and column variables; and ability to format output reports.
- *Statistical functions.* How easy is it to create the statistical analysis you need?

Profile of One Survey Package—TabHouse

TabHouse is a complete survey system for the Macintosh that originally ran on a mainframe. Unlike other software that has been transported from a mainframe environment, TabHouse has been completely recoded for the Macintosh. As a result, it fully uses many of the convenience-enhancing features of the graphic user interface.

TabHouse supports up to 32,000 variables, and can generate up to 32,000 banner columns. While this is probably more than most of us will

Survey Software

ever need, it means that this software is easily as powerful as that running on mainframe computers, and much more flexible.

The number of *records* or cases that can be analyzed is limited only by the amount of hard disk space available. The data can be read from a number of sources, such as spreadsheets or databases, and can use multiple data sets in the same analysis.

It also comes with a "proprietary data entry" (PDE) utility that allows you to create an electronic questionnaire to capture the data. No additional typing is needed to then prepare the data for analysis.

As every analyst knows, often it's not until you actually *see* your results that you know exactly the best way to look at them. You need to be able to play with the data to see what makes the most sense. TabHouse lets you do this on the fly. You can dynamically redefine variables until the exact cut you want is displayed.

For example, let's say you're doing a survey, and one of the variables is marital status. You allow four possible answers: married, widowed, divorced, and single. After you collect the data, you decide that based on the results a simple two-response break would do: married and unmarried, which includes the last three categories.

Redefining the data is done by using a LabelSet to, in effect, map the actual responses to combined categories created for the purposes of the analysis at hand. This is very easy to do, and makes the data really come alive when significant patterns are discovered.

The results of your analysis are also quite flexible. You can easily define and redefine what the columns and rows of your resulting tables are going to be. The program has many built-in statistics that can also be added flexibly. Formatting the output can also be done easily, in terms of fonts, type styles, and sizes.

Curiously, there is no graphic output available from this program. However, the analysis results can easily to exported to spreadsheets for further analysis, or to word processors or presentation software for preparation of project reports.

TabHouse includes some sophisticated features that put it in the major leagues:

- *Multiple responses.* Multiple responses are often valid, for example to the question "Which business magazines do you read

regularly?" TabHouse enables you to properly code these responses.
- *Concatenated variables.* Here's an anecdote that illustrates this feature. I recently had a client who wanted me to differentiate among the responses given by her customers versus non-customers in each of four business segments. In effect, I needed to combine the two variables. A concatenated or crossed variable enabled me to do this, by, in effect, creating eight segments instead of four. TabHouse creates up to three levels of these kinds of variables—more than adequate for most applications.
- *Table filters.* This allows you to filter certain responses out of your data before they are analyzed. In effect, this allows you to look at smaller segments of the data in greater detail. You might, for example, want to exclude from your analysis everyone who did not answer a particularly important question. TabHouse allows complex filtering based on up to two conditions—these may be in either *and* or *or* relationships to each other.

Major Survey Packages

	DOS	Windows	Macintosh
Survey Raosoft, Inc. 6645 Northeast Windermere Road Seattle, WA 98115 (206) 525-4025	●		
TabHouse Pericles Software 210 1/2 Louisiana Avenue Perrysburg, OH 43551 (419) 872-0966			●

Chapter Eighteen

Database Managers

In Chapter 16 we looked at commercial databases. Now we'll explore another use of the term *database*. In this chapter we use it to refer to software used to maintain a local, structured file—*not* an online database like we saw in Chapter 16. I've used the term database manager here to remind us of the distinction.

Basic Description of Database Management Software

Database software is the basic *record-keeping* software (much like spreadsheets are the basic *calculating* software.) Data is kept in *records*, with a record usually corresponding to one entity (a customer, for example). Each record contains several *fields*, which are the data elements that are kept on each entity (name, address and phone number, for example). The data is usually highly structured—that is, the same data elements are captured about each entity.

Databases specialize in *sorting* data in new ways and in *selecting* records based on a query input by the user. A question like "Find all my customers in New York City with account balances over $2,500 and credit lines over $7,500," which would take several person-months to calculate by hand, can be answered in seconds by a database—provided, of course, you have the data set up correctly in the first place.

Databases come in two basic flavors, *flat-file* and *relational*. Flat-file databases are generally simpler to use but are less flexible in their options. They are somewhat more capable than the database features within spreadsheets, which are simplified versions of flat-file databases.

Relational databases are complex, and can be made to do almost anything. The name *relational* comes from the fact that these databases can *link* data from two different files, thereby creating new data *relation-*

ships. They usually have powerful programming languages attached to them, which allow complex sets of commands and queries to be saved and easily executed later. These languages also allow *applications* to be developed in a way that the user is aware only of the application's functions, not the commands and operations of the underlying database.

The contact managers we looked at in Chapter 9 are essentially databases that do one thing only—manage customer and prospect lists. The databases we are discussing here are no more than raw materials that can be fashioned to do many useful things—if somebody has the skill and know-how to do so.

A database system typically consists of several types of computer files:

- *Data tables,* which contain the basic information
- *Query tables,* which contain parts of the information that have been filtered out based on a user request
- *Index files,* which keep the information in order
- *Screen files,* for data input and the like
- *Report files,* for printing the data in various formats
- *Procedural code files,* which tell the computer which computing operations to perform next

Marketing and Sales Applications for Database Managers

Marketing and sales applications abound for this kind of software, and are limited only by the needs of users and the capabilities of the database designers. Many times these packages are customized to meet a particular marketing need by an in-house applications developer or an outside consultant.

Sometimes customized database applications are so useful that they can be marketed themselves as stand-alone products that use a special version of the basic package called a *runtime* version. In many of these cases, the application marketer must pay a royalty to the publisher of the original database product.

Several uses for a database manager in marketing and sales are listed among the customized applications described in the case studies section. Some others include:

- Managing mailing and contact lists
- Analyzing survey data
- Customer segmentation analysis

Profile of One Package—Paradox

Paradox is a powerful relational database package for IBM-compatible machines. There are also Windows and OS/2 versions.

Paradox runs fast, even on very large files. It contains a complete programming language, called PAL ("Paradox Application Language"). The name Paradox is descriptive of the fact that while the software can easily be used by a newcomer to accomplish basic tasks, it has lots of features that keep the programming professionals happy as well.

Paradox pioneered a type of database searching called *query by example* that makes it relatively easy to get information back out of the database. Other programs have since emulated this time-saving feature.

Paradox enables you to "draw" input screens and forms, another feature that is a great convenience. You can create multi-color screens for data entry that include customized information, such as your company's name.

Customized reports are relatively easy to design. You can do cross-tabulations with Paradox, and can output numeric data in graphic form without exporting it to another program.

It is very easy to bring data created by another program into Paradox and to export Paradox data to another program.

Paradox includes an *applications generator* that enables programming novices to set up simple applications by just telling the computer what they want. Okay, it's a *little* more complicated than that but, if you're so inclined, this will help get you started in creating basic code. It's also a great way to learn the language—by watching how the application generator did what you asked it to do.

Paradox itself has a user interface that is similar to that of Lotus 1-2-3; as such, it has a familiar look and feel to many PC users. If you're designing an application using PAL, it is possible to totally insulate the user from the actual menu structure of the basic program, and to substitute a customized interface that you've designed. You can use the same terminology that people in your company use.

If you do create your own application, you can get an inexpensive runtime version of the program that enables other people who do not own Paradox to run your Paradox application.

Case Studies—Customized Applications

One of the great features of powerful relational databases is the degree to which they can be customized. The result appears to be a whole new application, with its own commands, input screens, and reports.

Paradox is a database that includes its own very flexible programming language. Each of the following is a Paradox application that the author designed, coded, and implemented at a major business services firm.

Response Management System

The opportunity here involved converting names of people requesting information about firm services into sales leads and, ultimately, into clients. This system is installed at the headquarters office, which handles fulfillment of all literature requests. All data about the request is entered at the time of the request, and fulfillment information is prepared. This information includes the shipping label for the information as well as reports to management that indicate which brochures are being requested most frequently.

At the end of the month, information on all requests for literature in each line of business is compiled. This information is sent in report format to the executive responsible for marketing that line of business. The executive can easily identify requests that look like promising leads, and make appropriate follow-up by mail and/or phone.

Collateral Inventory System

The problem here was that existing manual inventory controls for promotional materials (brochures, technical monographs, etc.) were slow and inaccurate. An inventory system was developed that tracks deletions from and additions to inventory at a central warehouse. The system provides inventory reconciliations between the warehouse and another distribution point where the materials are available.

Where the cost of the material shipped is to be charged back to the business unit on whose behalf the material is shipped, the system prepares an appropriate invoice automatically.

In addition to preventing stock-outs and ensuring that appropriate numbers of materials are ordered, the system creates management reports that assess demand for the various promotional and technical publications.

Clippings Tracking System

This is a system installed at the corporate communications office for classifying and tracking press clippings related to the firm's activities. Each month the firm's outside clipping service delivers a pile of clippings, culled from national, regional, and local news outlets and the trade press, that cite, quote or interview the firm's executives. This system enables some sense to be made out of that pile of information.

Each clipping is converted into an entry in the database that lists the following information:

- The executive cited, quoted, or interviewed
- The media outlet (name and type)
- The date of publication
- The topic of the citation
- Which (if any) of the firm's communications initiatives this clipping resulted from

Appearances on TV and radio are included. This system enables top management to be aware of geographic patterns of press attention, as well as trends over time. It enables the national and business unit communications officers to monitor the success of public relations campaigns.

Proposal Database

This firm has a group of professional writers in the headquarters office that assist local offices in developing major business proposals. The work done by this group is tracked in a database application that shows the following information:

- The date of the proposal
- The prospective client
- The industry classification of the prospect
- The services included in the proposal
- The writer(s) who worked on the proposal

- The firm office out of which the proposal was issued
- The fee amount of the proposal
- What other firms competed for this proposal
- The disposition of the proposal—won, lost, or pending

The result is a system that allows the group to monitor its own performance, to assign staff, and to report the results of its work to top management.

What to Look for in Database Software

Several factors will affect your choice of a database manager:

- *Complexity of task.* Your most basic choice is whether to use a flat-file or a relational database package. This will be determined by the complexity of the set of tasks you need the software to accomplish.
- *Speed.* If you're working with large files—say over 1,000 records—you'll want the speeds of various data manipulations to be acceptably fast.
- *Network-readiness.* If a group of people needs to access the same data over a local network, the software should be able to do this, and to have various file management features to make the data both easy to access and secure.
- *Ease of building queries.* How easy is it to get answers based on what you need to see? The database should also make it easy for you to *concatenate* queries, that is, to take the *results* of one query and make them the *subject* of the next query.
- *Quality of output.* Printouts vary significantly, with some databases offering *database publishing* quality of output. Database publishing is a hybrid of desktop publishing and database management. It is the term being given to the ability of some database management programs to produce camera-ready output for directories, catalogs, and other business communications.
- *Compatibility.* Database managers are often used to analyze data from other programs or even other computers. Mainframe data, for example, can be downloaded to most database managers. Although most database programs will import and export

data in various formats, you should be sure that the specific transfers you need to accomplish are feasible.

Major Flat-File Databases

	DOS	Windows	Macintosh
Filemaker Pro Claris Corporation 5201 Patrick Henry Drive Santa Clara, CA 95052 (408) 727-8227		●	●
Q&A Symantec Corporation 10201 Torre Avenue Cupertino, CA 95014 (800) 441-7234	●	●	●

Major Relational Databases

	DOS	Windows	Macintosh
Paradox Borland International 10 Victor Square Scotts Valley, CA 95067 (408) 438-8400	●	●	
Access Microsoft Corporation 1 Microsoft Way Redmond, WA 98052-6399 (206) 882-8080		●	
Fourth Dimension ACIUS Inc. 10351 Bubb Road Cupertino, CA 95014 (408) 252-4444			●

Chapter Nineteen

Scanner Data Analysis

A continually greater number of transactions at supermarkets and other retail stores are captured by point-of-sale scanners. Scanner data is used by the store for pricing items at the time of sale and for maintaining inventory records.

The data is also captured, aggregated, and fed back on a daily basis to a large central computer for further aggregation and analysis. The results of scanner data analysis used to be delivered to brand managers—days or weeks later—in thick printouts. Now there are ways to get it virtually in "real time" in electronic form.

Basic Description of Scanner Data Analysis Software

Scanner data analysis (SDA) software is designed specifically for interactively analyzing the huge amounts of data generated by point-of-sale scanners. It is designed to be used by managers in consumer packaged goods manufacturing and by retailers.

To use the software, you must first have access to the scanner data. Scanner data is supplied mainly by two companies, A.C. Nielsen and Information Resources, Inc. As you might guess, the front-end software to analyze this data is also supplied by those two companies.

Scanner data contracts are expensive, often well into six figures per year, and sometimes over $1 million. But packaged goods companies live and die by these numbers—they have immense value in allocating promotional and advertising spending.

SDA software is, in effect, a version of an executive information system (EIS—see Chapter 22) tailored specifically to work with scanner data as a source. As with any EIS, other internal data can be brought into the analysis as well.

The software may contain other modules as well, such as a word processor, a spreadsheet, and a presentation package. The results of the analysis can also be exported to a stand-alone software package.

Benefits of Scanner Data Analysis Software

SDA software enables faster, more effective use to be made of scanner data. Instead of getting reams of printouts to wade through, the analyst can quickly call up a particular piece of data. The time saved in getting to the data can be spent exploring and testing it.

Marketing and Sales Applications for Scanner Data Analysis Software

SDA software's *only* applications are in sales and marketing. Scanner data analysis can be used for:

- Reviewing category and brand performance
- Evaluating the effects of special promotions
- Evaluating the effects of advertising
- Test marketing new products
- Identifying new distribution opportunities

Example—Competitive Intelligence

Here's a hypothetical example of how such a system could be used. Let's say you're a brand manager for a nationally recognized cold remedy. You've heard through the grapevine that one of your biggest competitors is in trouble, and you want to check into it.

Using SDA software, you call up national sales data for the cold remedy category. This tells you that national sales for the whole category are up almost 15 percent during the current four-week period.

But you can also drill down though the data to look at one brand or one market. In this case you can quickly isolate the data for just your competitor's brand—and see that it's down significantly. Then you can

Scanner Data Analysis

do a geographic break, and see if this poor performance is a national trend or is just occurring in selected markets.

Profile of One SDA Package—Nielsen Workstation

The Nielsen Workstation is a leader in the SDA field. It is marketed by Nielsen Marketing Research, an affiliate of the Nielsen television ratings organization, which is now part of Dun & Bradstreet.

The Workstation began life in Europe as the INF*ACT Workstation, which claims over 1,000 companies as users. The product has three types of users:

- Brand managers and product managers
- Market research and information people
- The sales force—from vice presidents to account reps

Workstation runs under Windows, and takes complete advantage of the icon-driven interface—many operations can be completed literally at the click of a mouse button. It makes use of *data visualization*, the power of pictures to make sense of large amounts of data. Patterns and trends can be spotted more readily this way than they can be in pages of printouts.

The Workstation accesses and integrates various types of data:

- Scanner data from Nielsen's 3,000-store SCANTRACK Service
- Data from Nielsen's 40,000 household SCANTRACK National Electronic Household Panel
- Internal company sales and product shipment records

Workstation enables you to quickly identify exceptional activity by using color-coded graphics. It allows you to rapidly prepare reports describing:

- Which brands in a category increased share the most
- Which brands lost share
- The markets with the largest share swings
- Details on pricing, distribution, and other variables

Major Packages

	DOS	Windows	Macintosh
Nielsen Workstation Nielsen Marketing Research Nielsen Plaza Northbrook, IL 60062-6288 (708) 498-6300		●	

Chapter Twenty

Multimedia

Computer data is a lot more than numbers and letters. Digital technology has been harnessed to capture things that seem essentially non-numeric, like sound and graphic images. Advances in hardware technology are enabling these kinds of images to be integrated and manipulated on a desktop computer. This exciting new development will bring us many new products and capabilities in the next few years.

Basic Description of Multimedia Software

Multimedia software combines sound, graphics, animation, and video into one presentation format. It has the potential of evolving into its own communications medium. Its commercial applications generally fall into two categories:

- *Home entertainment and education.* Various interactive games are beginning to be released in this format, and there are several reference works (formerly books) now available.
- *Corporate training.* At this writing this is the main application for multimedia in the business world.

Most multimedia applications run on CD-ROM (compact disk, read-only memory) disks. While there is nothing intrinsic to multimedia that requires this format, the large amounts of disk space required to store visual and sound data make it a practical necessity. A CD-ROM holds about 600 megabytes of data, about 400 times what a high-density floppy disk holds. Even some nonmultimedia software applications have become so complex that they are new being released in both floppy disk and CD-ROM formats.

The price of CD-ROM players has fallen below $500, and at this writing there are over 3,000 CD-ROM software titles commercially available. Yet this technology hasn't really caught on, in either the business or the consumer environments.

This could change quickly. For example, if one "must have" application comes along that requires a CD-ROM drive, that by itself could stabilize the market quickly.

The other main thing holding back market acceptance is that multimedia requires a "souped up" PC in order to operate. In addition to the CD-ROM drive, you have to have good graphics, enhanced sound capabilities, and the capacity to run Windows. (I'm speaking here of IBM-compatible machines. Several Macintosh models are equipped to run multimedia out of the box.)

Collectively, the requirements for a PC to run multimedia applications are known as MPC specifications. The MPC specifications were developed by the Multimedia PC Marketing Council, an industry consortium. They include the following minimum requirements for running an MPC-format application:

- A 386-based PC
- 2 megabytes of RAM
- A 30 megabyte hard disk
- A CD-ROM drive capable of a sustained transfer rate of at least 150 kilobytes per second
- A VGA or better color screen
- 8-bit digitized sound and MIDI (Musical Instruments Digital Interface) playback
- Stereo speakers
- Microsoft Windows 3.1

While almost all new IBM compatibles, with the addition of a CD-ROM drive, a sound board, and speakers meet these requirements, most older machines do not—and cannot, even with retrofits. You have to start over.

The other big drawback of CD-ROMs is that, as their name states, they are "read only." (Their full name is Compact Disk Read Only Memory.) This means that while you can pull information off them, you can't "write" or store new information. It's a one-way medium at this point.

The only way to write to CD-ROM format is to have expensive *mastering* equipment available—and then it can only be done once per disk. Some corporations have begun to distribute internal information this way.

Marketing and Sales Applications for Multimedia

At this point multimedia is not a core marketing application for PC technology, yet I believe its future in marketing is promising. Its value is that it is *interactive*. At any juncture in a CD-ROM presentation, you can be presented with a choice button that allows you to send the presentation down one fork or another. In the games that are coming out now, this means, for example, that you can choose from among alternative endings for a mystery story.

What it will mean for marketers is a medium that can respond to an individual customer's unique needs and interests. Many of us talk about becoming more market-driven, and this will help us do so.

Here are some examples of what this could mean:

- *Sales presentations.* Rather than a static slide show or video presentation, a salesperson could literally respond to the interests and concerns of her customer or prospect on the spot. This could mean a more consistent presentation and response across the entire sales force.
- *Sales training.* Following from the above, training modules could be developed for salespeople. These might include specifications on newly introduced products, commonly encountered prospect objections, etc.
- *Video catalogs.* These will allow you to search for items that you're most interested in, then to see them in full still or moving video. Product specifications can be called up with a keystroke, and the product can be customized by the consumer to his exact specifications.
- *Mailers.* Like catalogs, product demonstrations could be put into disk format and sent as direct mail pieces, like sometimes is done with videotapes. This was done in the premultimedia 1980s by several automobile manufacturers using floppy disks. The results look crude now, but the new technology makes this an approach worth revisiting.

- *Advertising storyboards.* TV ads can be dummied up in multi-media format before expensive commitments to production facilities and personnel are made. See the case study below.

Video

A recent development is the ability to include video clips in a multi-media presentation. This is a sensational effect, as graphic borders can be created in other programs to frame the video.

There is an extension to the Macintosh operating system called Quick-Time that enables all of this to happen. Video for Windows is the IBM compatible equivalent.

In addition, you need a hardware board compatible with your computer to translate the images from videotape to digital format. One of these is called VideoSpigot.

VideoSpigot
SuperMac Technology
485 Potrero Avenue
Sunnyvale, CA 94086
(800) 334-3005

Case Study—An Electronic Storyboard

A developer recently showed me a program he had developed in Hyper-Card for an advertising agency. This custom application supported storyboard development for a TV advertisement. First still art was created to represent the visual part of the ad. About thirty stills were needed for a 60-second ad. Voice-overs were recorded on the Macintosh hard disk in synch with the visuals.

The whole thing was then scripted so that it ran in real time by itself at roughly the speed that it was anticipated to run in the final ad. It was presented to the client for his reaction at this point. It was relatively easy to change things, since nothing had yet been committed to film.

Once a final version of this "living" storyboard was created, the application was used to control the actual shooting of the commercial. In order to save on production costs, the ad was being shot in Mexico. Most of the actors did not speak English well.

The sequenced electronic storyboard was played for the actors, and they were able to learn much of what to do from watching the screen. A great savings was achieved in the overall production costs of the ad.

Major Multi-Media Authoring Packages

	DOS	Windows	Macintosh
Macromind Director Macromedia, Inc. 600 Townsend Street San Francisco, CA 94103 (415) 442-0200			●
Action Macromedia, Inc. 600 Townsend Street San Francisco, CA 94103 (415) 442-0200		●	

Chapter Twenty-One

Project Managers and Timekeepers

In this chapter we'll discuss two separate, but closely related, kinds of software: project managers and timekeepers. They both track large, complex projects, measure progress against goals, and measure spending against budgets.

Basic Description of Project Management Software

Project management software does the following things:

- Tracks a list of tasks and subtasks to be completed as part of a project.
- Tracks dependencies between the tasks. For example, the page layout must be done before the brochure goes to the printer.
- Tracks the person or people responsible for each task.
- Tracks the resource time (person-hours) required for each task.
- Tracks the calendar time for each task—the milestone date by which it must be finished.
  Actual times can be entered and compared with the planned times. Slippage in the delivery date of a task can be addressed by (a) moving the due dates of later dependent tasks, or (b) adding other resources to keep the dates intact.
- Tracks the dollar costs associated with each task. Again, actuals can be entered and compared with the plan.

Many of these programs were designed to manage extremely complex tasks, with hundreds or thousands of steps, and intricate task dependency relationships. There are some programs, however, that are designed for less complex projects.

Basic Description of Timekeeping Software

Timekeeping software enables you to track actual time being spent against a project plan. It is often used by professionals who charge for their time, like lawyers and management consultants. The software aggregates time spent—often with several people inputting time data over a network—against project or client codes. Out-of-pocket costs can also be tracked back to individual clients.

Benefits of Using Project Management and Timekeeping Software

The benefits of detailed project planning include the following:

- The planning process itself forces you to think through all the steps involved in completing a project, and their relationships to each other.
- Once a project plan is set, you can monitor the actual course of the project against completion dates and budgets. You'll know quickly if you're going to be late or over budget, and can make adjustments to other parts of the project to correct that.
- It helps communicate the complexity of the project. For example, things like lead times for media placements and collateral production may not be familiar to product managers and other clients. By diagramming all of the steps involved, project management software allows you to graphically educate your audience, and thereby manage their expectations.
- Tracking of project actuals against plans (time and budget) can help make planning for future similar projects more realistic, since they can be based on experience. Done well, this can become the basis of organizational learning—it enables you to do your projections a little better each time.

Marketing and Sales Applications for Project Management Software

Project management software can be used in several marketing contexts:

- *Managing complex projects.* These might include the development of advertising campaigns, product roll-outs, research efforts, and so on.
- *Selling complex projects.* In a business-to-business sale of a complex project (a consulting engagement, for example), laying out the project during its design phase can help clients understand the complexity of the effort—and convince them to be willing to pay for it!

Marketing and Sales Applications for Timekeeping Software

Timekeeping software can be used for:

- Sales force management
- Accruing professional time charges in a professional practice (law firm, market research company, etc.)

What to Look for in Project Management Software

Several factors should guide your selection of a project management package:

- *Ease of use.* The newer generation of project managers takes full advantage of the graphic user interface afforded by both the Macintosh and Windows environments. These generally make it much easier to set dependencies and task durations.
- *Complexity.* Some of these packages were literally developed for rocket scientists at NASA. This is overkill for many marketing programs, which are relatively simple. There are project managers that are less complex, and easier to master, that may be more appropriate.

Profile of One Project Management Package—Timeline

Timeline is the leading project manager for the IBM PC and compatibles. It has just been revised. The latest version has graphics output that is nothing short of stunning. It supports printers and other devices like image recorders (for making presentation-quality 35 mm slides.)

Timeline uses an outline format for entering tasks. This helps users keep track of their priorities, and is easy to use and edit. Timeline's user interface is graphic, and it supports a mouse. This makes it easy to move due dates, for example, by physically moving pointers on the screen. The interface is not Windows-based, though, and probably will be eclipsed for project managers once the Windows standard is established.

Timeline's manual is excellent and includes introductory information on the concepts of project management. There is also a disk-based tutorial that helps you get started using the product.

The program is extremely flexible, therefore complex to operate. If you don't know what a Gantt chart is, don't attempt this one on your own.

One drawback: if your resource schedules are idiosyncratic, Timeline may not meet your needs. A colleague of mine found that because his staffers work different days and hours, Timeline's lack of individual resource calendars was difficult to live with.

Profile of One Timekeeping Package—Timeslips

At this writing, TimeSlips, a very sophisticated electronic stopwatch, is the only program of its kind and therefore virtually defines the category. Though primarily designed for recording the time of professionals in professional services firms (like law firms), the approach is equally applicable to project management and sales force management.

TimeSlips actually consists of two linked programs, TSTimer and TSReports. TSTimer is the input side of the software. It captures what person is doing the work, which client the work is for, what project the work relates to, and exactly what was done. It reads the system clock of the computer, and is ideal for the professional with ready access to a PC to log in work as it is done. It can be kept memory resident, so it is available at the touch of a hot key in the middle of another computing activity. It links to underlying databases of professionals, their billing rates, clients, and projects.

Project Managers and Timekeepers 163

TSReports is the output side of the software. It reports accumulated time charges, creates extensions based on billing rates, creates invoices, ages receivables, reviews account histories, and tracks chargeable activity by professional. It exports files to Dbase or Lotus 1-2-3 for further analysis, or to word processors for further formatting.

Invoices and management reports can be customized by the user. Several choices are available to the user as to how much detail will appear on the invoice. A macro recorder and some basic graphics are also provided.

Both hourly and flat rate billing are supported. Hourly charges can be based on who did the work, whom it was done for, or what kind of work was done. Out-of-pocket expenses are tracked separately.

Several add-on products are available for additional cost. One enables you to link TimeSlips to your general accounting software. Another spell-checks your invoices. Another enables several professionals to do data entry, with invoices later produced centrally.

Major Project Management Packages

	DOS	Windows	Macintosh
Timeline Symantec Corporation 10201 Torre Avenue Cupertino, CA 95014 (800) 441-7234	●		
Microsoft Project Microsoft Corporation 1 Microsoft Way Redmond, WA 98052-6399 (206) 882-8080		●	●

Major Timekeeping Package

	DOS	Windows	Macintosh
TimeSlips TimeSlips Corporation 239 Western Avenue Essex, MA 01929 (800) 285-0999	●	●	●

Chapter Twenty-Two

Other Software

There are other kinds of commercial software that marketers should know about. While none of these is used so extensively in marketing that it deserves its own chapter, they are nevertheless worthy of note.

Thought Processors

Basic Description of Thought Processing Software

Thought processing is an artificial-intelligence-like activity that serves as a personal assistant for brainstorming and problem solving. To my knowledge there is only one package like this commercially available, IdeaFisher. The description that follows applies directly to that package.

This software consists of two large databases:

- QBank, which contains nearly 6,000 questions
- IdeaBank, which contains over 60,000 words and phrases

These databases can generate over 700,000 different linkages, depending on what you tell them to do. They help stimulate your thinking by generating free-association connections for you to consider.

You start using the software in the QBank mode. You can ask three types of questions: orient/clarify, modify, or evaluate. The questions themselves are organized into categories, such as marketing strategy ideas, or ideas for a screenplay.

You answer each of the questions that the software poses to you. For example, in designing a marketing campaign, questions could include the following:

- Are your prospective customers already familiar with this kind of product, or must you sell them on the idea itself?
- What drives sales in this market (such as impulse, quality, price, reputation, on-site service, availability, or parts)?
- What angle does this suggest for the advertising?
- What position does the product hold in people's thinking about this type of product? In other words, what is this product known as?

The software uses the answers to these questions to present you with ideas from the IdeaBank. Not all of these, or course, are relevant. You pull those that are relevant out of the list and into the program's simple word processor.

You can add your own entries to either the question base or the idea base.

Benefits of Thought Processing Software

IdeaFisher is a thinking assistant. It helps you remember associations that might take longer to come up with without it. It therefore can save time when you need to come up with something new.

Marketing and Sales Applications for Thought Processing

Some of the ways that this software can be used include:

- *Writing copy.* Advertising or direct mail copy can be kick-started with this software.
- *Naming new products or services.* Many successful product names have some associative relationship to the product and/or its benefits.
- *Strategic planning.* The company offers an extra-cost Strategic Planning Module designed specifically for this purpose.
- *Writing presentations.* The company offers another option, the Presentation Planning Module, for this purpose.

Other Software   167

Major Thought Processing Package

	DOS	Windows	Macintosh
IdeaFisher Fisher Idea Systems 2222 Martin Street, Suite 110 Irvine, CA 92715 (800) 289-4332	●		●

Text Retrieval

Basic Description of Text Retrieval Software

Text retrieval software is also known as *textbase* software. A textbase, not surprisingly, is a collection of text material, as a database is a collection of data. Texts may be notes, articles, letters, or any other collections of words. The textbase is typically very loosely structured, or unstructured. Text retrieval software usually incorporates some combination of the following features:

- *Keyword search.* The ability to index texts on significant words contained in the text.
- *Full text search.* The ability to search for and display quickly all texts containing certain words or phrases.
- *Hypertext.* This fascinating feature has gotten a big boost lately thanks to the introduction of HyperCard, a Macintosh product that is bundled with each Mac. Hypertext is a technology that allows the user to "drill down" though information according to its meaning, not according to its sequential order on the screen. It's basically a dynamic index that allows information to be cross-referenced and accessed according to the needs of the user, not the writer.
- *Outlining.* The ability to collapse texts into outlines, or to build up texts by first constructing outlines.

There is a variety of sources for information that might be managed with text retrieval software. These include:

- *Keyed input.* Data input the old fashioned way, by pounding at the keyboard.

- *Existing electronic documents.* Word processing documents, for example, that are already in digital format. Spreadsheets and electronic databases can also be accessed in this manner.
- *Online searches.* Most professional communications software allows the results of an electronic database search to be "logged to disk." This means that you've captured the results of your search on disk, so that you can search and format it later.
- *Electronic mail.* Similarly, electronic mail can be retrieved to disk for filing purposes.
- *Scanned images and documents.* This technology allows typed or printed documents to be electronically read into digital form.
- *Optical disk.* Although this technology is currently managed by its own proprietary technologies, it's a reasonable guess that text retrieval concepts will sooner or later be applied to these massive collections of data.

Most current programs in this category simply find all the instances of a particular keyword. If this results in a large number of "hits," they will be presented to you by the software, usually in alphabetical order. You must then review each article to determine its true relevance to your query.

The latest innovation here is called *weighted relevance*. Software packages that have this feature will be able to *rank* what they find based on the content of each file. This will enable you to quickly locate the files that most likely are the most relevant.

Benefits of Text Retrieval Software

Text retrieval software enables you to:

- Categorize and organize large amounts of information
- Find what you want quickly out of a large body of archived information

Hard disks are now routinely offered in the 300-500 megabyte range. Compact disks are even larger than this, and the ability to find information quickly can provide a competitive edge.

This kind of software has been used extensively in the legal arena. One package was used to organize the volumes of testimony produced

Other Software 169

during the Iran-Contra hearings. Another package was used by a legal publisher to convert a 15-volume set of law books into one CD-ROM.

Marketing and Sales Applications for Text Retrieval Software

Competitor analysis is the only marketing-related application of this kind of software that I'm aware of. It has been used to classify and analyze competitor materials such as:

- Print advertisements
- Broadcast advertisements (using transcripts)
- Announcement of executive changes
- Newspaper and magazine clippings provided by clipping services
- The results of online searches

Major Text Retrieval Packages

	DOS	Windows	Macintosh
Folio Views Folio Corporation 2155 North Freedom Boulevard Suite 150 Provo, UT 84604 (800) 523-3034	●		
Sonar Professional Virginia Systems 5509 West Bay Court Midlothina, VA 23112 (804) 739-3200		●	●

Executive Information Systems (EIS)

Basic Description of EIS Software

Executive Information Systems (EIS) are systems that gather data from a number of types of sources, then integrate them into summary reports, usually for top management. The reports are presented on-screen, and the viewer is provided the opportunity to "drill down" though the summary data to see exactly where it came from.

These kinds of systems were originally developed for mainframe computers. Several systems now exist for PC networks, and these are much more flexible and less expensive than their mainframe counterparts.

Benefits of EIS Software

A good EIS creates a true management information system. The key information that management needs to run the business is routinely gathered and organized by the system. Management can "work the numbers" interactively and thereby get more true information out of the data.

As shown in the example below, EIS output can also help in working with suppliers or distribution channels.

Marketing and Sales Applications for EIS

EIS software is often the platform for marketing information systems, which gather marketing and sales information from a number of sources.

The Dr Pepper/7Up Companies, for example, use an EIS to give upper management sales and demographic data.[1] Dr Pepper has replaced paper reports with electronic reports distributed over a PC network. At the end of each month, the people at Dallas headquarters generate electronic files out of their PowerPlay EIS. These are distributed over the network to the local offices.

Local office executives can then review the sales performance of the bottlers in their region. They can even load the files on to a portable PC, then review the files interactively with the bottler's executives on site.

Major EIS Packages

	DOS	Windows	Macintosh
Forest & Trees Channel Computing, Inc. 53 Main Street Newmarket, NH 03857 (800) 289-0053	●	●	
PowerPlay Cognos, Inc. 67 South Bedford Street Burlington, MA 01803 (617) 229-6600	●		

Electronic Bulletin Boards (BBS)

Basic Description of the Software

Electronic bulletin board systems (BBS) allow you to create and maintain your own private online systems (see Chapter 16). They offer many of the same functions as commercial online systems, including electronic mail, file downloading, and electronic conferencing. In addition, some BBS systems offer fax-back capabilities for distributing information to callers' fax machines (see Chapter 6).

BBS systems are, of course, simpler and much less powerful than commercial systems, which typically run on networks of mainframe computers. BBS systems have for years been used by computer enthusiasts to exchange software, commentary and technical information. Now they are also being used in the corporate world.

BBS systems are fairly complicated to set up and require someone (the system operator, or *sysop*) to maintain them. Depending on the complexity of the BBS software and the number of users, this can get to be a full-time job. This and any other maintenance costs must be factored into the equation if you're considering this kind of software.

Alternatively, several online services (CompuServe, for example) provide private bulletin board and conferencing services for a fee. Depending on the volume of messaging you expect, this may be a less expensive approach.

Benefits of BBS Software

The key benefit here is being able to distribute information quickly to anyone, anywhere in the world, who has a computer and a modem. Some users report using BBS systems as an alternative to direct dial-in to their company's LAN. This is because security breaches on a LAN can be quite serious, leading for example to computer virus infections or unauthorized viewing of, or tampering with, files. A BBS can allow people to have access to your company, and still insulate you from pranksters and computer felons.

Marketing and Sales Applications for Bulletin Board Systems

BBS systems provide much of the same functionality as e-mail and other online systems. They can be used for:

- Customer communications and support
- Distribution channel communications and support
- Sales force automation
- Order entry and processing

Profile of One Bulletin Board System— American Business Research Network

A bulletin board of particular interest to market researchers is the American Business Research Network. This is an electronic information catalog that can be accessed—free—by anyone with a modem. It contains listings of several hundred marketing-related books and research reports. Their costs range from less than $30 to more than $2,000, and they can be ordered online using an American Express card.

The books and reports are classified by category. They include high-quality reports on whole industries, as well as reports on companies. The former are produced by research companies like Market Intelligence. The latter are produced by investment analysts at PaineWebber and Sanford Bernstein.

You can view the complete directory—and download it for printing out later—at no charge.

American Business Research Network, Inc.
203 Commack Road, Suite 135
Commack, NY 11725-3401
(516) 754-9144 - voice/fax
(516) 754-9205 - modem (N/8/1)

Major Bulletin Board Packages

	DOS	Windows	Macintosh
NovaLink Pro **Resnova Software Inc.** **16458 Bolsa Chica Street** **Unit 193** **Huntington Beach, CA 92649** **(714) 840-6082**			●
PC Board **Clark Development Company, Inc.** **PO Box 71365** **Murray, UT 84107** **(800) 356-1686**	●		

Document Assembly

Basic Description of Document Assembly Software

Document assembly software enables the user to create customized documents quickly and easily. By answering a series of questions, the user provides input to the software. The software then uses a library of preformatted text to construct a completed, seamless document that reflects all of that input.

Document assembly is a burgeoning software application that probably is most applicable in the legal field, where it can be used to create contracts and other legal documents. There is, for example, a program (WillMaker from Nolo Press) that constructs simple wills legal in 49 states. You enter information about what you wish to leave to whom, and the program does the rest. It even adds language required to be in wills in your particular state of residence.

There is similar software to do this for employee policy manuals (Policies Write Now! from Knowledge Point) and for job descriptions (Descriptions Write Now!, also from Knowledge Point).

Tax preparation software is probably the most widely used segment of the document-assembly market.

Benefits of Document Assembly Software

Document assembly software can be used to create complex documents quickly and easily. Some experts have predicted that most legal documents will be prepared this way in the not-too-distant future.

The basic benefit is the time saved in copying such a document. Particularly when this is expensive professional time (a lawyer or a senior marketing professional), the savings can be substantial.

The other primary benefit is the completeness and quality of the document. A document assembly program tells you when your document needs more information to be complete. This helps reduce errors and can reduce training time for the personnel using the document.

Marketing and Sales Applications for Document Assembly Software

Document assembly is potentially applicable every time a document is created. In marketing, it could be used for:

- *Database marketing.* This is a form of direct marketing in which the message is tailored to the individual target, based for example on information specific to her or his account.
- *Business proposals and marketing plans.* These often must contain essentially the same *types* of information, though the content of each must, of course, be customized.
- *Credit applications.* When making a sale depends on getting credit, a credit application can be customized very quickly using this software.
- *Account applications.* Similarly, other kinds of account applications (like mortgage applications) could be prepared quickly by this kind of software. Because of the portability of both PCs and printers, this can be done in the field (even at the customer's residence).

Major Document Assembly Packages

Many document assembly applications are proprietary, and must be custom designed by software developers for the companies that use them.

I am not aware of any commercially available document assembly package applicable to marketing situations.

Artificial Intelligence

Artificial intelligence is the mimicking of human reasoning through various computer technologies. One of the most widely used of these technologies is *expert systems*. Expert systems pool the accumulated expertise and problem-solving patterns of real-world experts into a knowledge base governed by a set of internal logic rules.

Expert systems are most widely used for solving technical problems. Their main marketing-related application to date is in the area of *customer service*. Many companies, particularly those that sell consumer products, have toll-free numbers for purchasers to call for questions about the product or problems with the product.

These hot lines are staffed by small armies of customer-service representatives, each of whom takes calls hour after hour. Some questions require considerable expertise to answer. For example, one food manufacturer has to deal with complex questions on ingredients ("Does this product contain any complex sugar? I'm allergic to it.") and consumer problems ("One half hour after eating your product, my face and hands swelled up.")

Training customer service representatives is expensive, and this company felt that it would be impossible to ask any rep to master all of the different situations that he or she could potentially encounter.

So they developed an expert system that allowed many of the more common problems to be answered on the spot. Following the example above, the rep types "swelling" into the system, which then prompts the rep to ask the caller whether he or she drank milk along with eating the product. A "yes" answer reveals that in 10 percent of the population, eating this product with milk causes swelling of the face and hands. Appropriate advice can be given to the caller.

These systems are often used to speed diagnostics, thereby improving customer service. Auto repair, for example, would be a great application—one that could be sold to shops and directly to do-it-yourselfers.

Electronic Data Interchange (EDI)

Electronic data interchange (EDI) links suppliers and their business customers for ordering, billing, and inventory purposes. This is often used, for example, between clothing retailers and manufacturers. Purchase orders are sent via modem or directly linked terminals (via "leased lines") to the supplier, and the supplier sends the invoice by return EDI. Sometimes electronic payment back to the supplier is sent by electronic funds transfer.

More advanced EDI systems have an *automatic replenishment* feature that links to the inventory system of the buying company. When the system shows (via scanner data from the point of sale) that size 10 red dresses are low, the system *automatically* generates a purchase order for more dresses from the manufacturer's system. This is particularly valuable for companies that want to keep inventories as low as possible, yet have enough on hand not to lose orders (*just-in-time inventory*).

EDI is important from a marketing point of view when having items in stock is key to making the sale. This is particularly true of most retail sales situations. EDI creates a seamless boundary between companies, which itself comes near the essence of marketing.

EDI is a business-to-business technology, not one for small businesses or individuals. Fax technology, which of course *is* within reach, has been called "the poor man's EDI" because of its ability to mimic some of the features of true EDI, at far lower cost.

Endnote

1. Jim Kinlan, "EIS in the Real World," *Byte Magazine,* June 1992: 210-211.

PART THREE

APPLYING THE TOOLS

Chapter Twenty-Three

A Day in the Life

That concludes the tour. Now, what have we seen? And more important, how does this all fit into an average day in the life of a typical marketing or sales professional?

In this chapter I've taken a functional look at a generic marketing and sales process, and mapped each part of that process back to technologies most likely to benefit it. It's basically a cross-reference to Chapters 3 through 22, each of which describes a particular set of information technologies. Each part of the basic sales/marketing process is listed, along with a list of the technologies most likely to be applied to it.

If there's any part of the process that particularly interests you, find it below and note the technologies that address it. Then you can go back to the previous chapters that focus on those technologies.

Note that I've spoken in terms of a sales and marketing *process*. In larger organizations the organizational structure may resemble this process, with a different unit for each part of the process. In smaller companies, there's more likely to be significant overlap in terms of the number of segments of the process managed by a particular functional unit. If you're on your own, of course, you do it all.

Here's how I've outlined the generic sales/marketing process:

Marketing
    Market research
    Competitive analysis
    Advertising
    Direct marketing
    Public relations

Sales
    Leads management
    Relationship building
    Making the sale
    Customer and channel support

Sales support
    Sales training
    Sales force management
    Sales analysis and forecasting

Now I'll identify technologies that may be applicable to each phase of that process.

Marketing

Market Research

- *Survey software.* Survey software can help in the design, execution, and analysis of both telephone and mail surveys (Chapter 17).
- *Fax.* Companies are beginning to conduct surveys by fax, rather than mail. Preliminary studies show that the level of response is higher than for mail, and the responses are made on average more quickly (Chapter 6).
- *Voice mail.* A desktop voice mail system can conduct a survey that prompts respondents to answer by pushing touch-tone buttons, or recording voice responses (Chapter 7).
- *E-mail.* It is possible to use electronic mail, including the e-mail component of groupware, to conduct surveys (Chapter 12).
- *Desktop publishing.* Respondents to mail surveys like to have something visually appealing to respond to. For phone surveys, a well-organized, professional-looking questionnaire promotes clear responses and builds morale among the interviewers (Chapter 5).
- *Spreadsheets.* Spreadsheets can be used to further analyze and chart tabulation data produced by either a desktop system or by a mainframe computer (Chapter 15).

A Day in the Life

- *Mailing lists managers.* For distributing mail surveys, or for developing samples for telephone surveys (Chapter 4).

Competitive Analysis

- *Online databases.* Online databases are windows on the world, and form the core of a competitive analyst's arsenal (Chapter 16).
- *Database managers.* Database managers can be used to track structured information known about competitors (Chapter 18).
- *Text retrieval.* Text retrieval software can be used to organize and analyze the massive amounts of material that may result from online searching (Chapter 22).

Advertising

- *Desktop publishing.* Simple print ads can be laid out using desktop publishing software (Chapter 5).
- *Spreadsheets.* Spreadsheets software can be used to determine optimal media placements and schedules (Chapter 15).
- *Project managers.* Project managers can be used to keep complex projects such as advertising schedules, on track (Chapter 21).
- *Thought processors.* These brainstorming assistants can help when designing new positioning, product names, or advertising approaches (Chapter 22).
- *Multimedia.* Advertising storyboards are now being created using multimedia software. In the near future, it is likely that multimedia may itself become an advertising medium, as videotape has become (Chapter 20).

Direct Marketing (Direct Mail and Telemarketing)

- *Mailing list managers.* Direct mail can be more personalized and targeted using desktop mailing list software (Chapter 4).
- *Contact managers.* Contact managers can be used to do direct mail, and can be used for telemarketing campaigns (Chapter 9).

- *Word processors.* Most word processors contain mail merge, a feature that can be used to generate simple direct mailings Chapter 3).
- *Desktop publishing.* More sophisticated mailing pieces, including company and product brochures, can be generated by a desktop publishing program (Chapter 5).
- *Fax.* Although fax could potentially be a significant technology in direct marketing, it is unclear at this point how legislative efforts to prevent this will develop (Chapter 6).
- *Online databases.* Online searches can used to identify and screen companies for further direct marketing efforts (Chapter 16).

Public Relations

- *Online databases.* Online databases can be used to distribute one's own press releases. They can also be used to identify emerging issues that the company needs to be on top of (Chapter 16).
- *Mailing list managers.* Mailing lists can be used to distribute press releases efficiently to targeted media outlets (Chapter 4).
- *Contact management.* Contact managers can be used to distribute press releases and to make phone follow-ups (Chapter 9).
- *Database managers.* Desktop database managers can be used to track press coverage and thereby measure the effectiveness of the PR function (Chapter 18).
- *Groupware.* Groupware can be used to quickly build the consensus needed to make a rapid response to a breaking news story (Chapter 13).
- *Fax.* Broadcast fax can be used to quickly distribute press releases to many media outlets (Chapter 6).

Sales

Leads Management

- *Online databases.* Online databases, and similar databases on CD-ROM, are very useful in generating lists of businesses or end consumers (Chapter 16).
- *Contact managers.* Contact managers are useful in qualifying leads (usually done by telephone) and in building them into relationships (Chapter 9).
- *Sales force automation.* Sales force automation software often assists in the assigning of leads generated through direct mail or through direct-response advertising to field salespeople for qualifying and follow-up (Chapter 10).

Relationship Building

- *Contact managers.* Contact managers are a great help in maintaining contact with key accounts and prospects (Chapter 9).
- *Time managers.* Time managers can help in the scheduling of appointments and can be used as electronic tickler files to monitor follow-up (Chapter 8).
- *Electronic bulletin boards.* Bulletin board systems can be used to build relationships with end users and with distribution channels (Chapter 22).

Making the Sale

- *Presentation software.* Once you're in a prospect's office, a good presentation of your company and its product or services can seal the deal. It's particularly persuasive if it is customized to address the unique needs of that client company or individual (Chapter 14).
- *Multimedia.* In the near future sales presentations will probably be enhanced by some form of laptop-based interactive multimedia (Chapter 20).
- *Document assembly.* In cases where the service involves a detailed application or some other document (like some financial

services), the sales process can be speeded up by having a custom document created on the spot (Chapter 22).

Customer and Channel Support

- *Expert systems.* Expert systems can help customer support representatives diagnose and respond to customers' and dealers' questions and problems (Chapter 22).
- *Electronic bulletin boards.* Electronic bulletin boards and the bulletin board features of online databases are being used to inform customers and dealers of product availability and pricing, as well as to provide solutions to problems and questions (Chapter 22).

Sales Support

Sales Training

- *Desktop publishing.* High-quality training materials help motivate the sales force. This includes materials used to introduce new products and promotions (Chapter 5).
- *Presentation software.* Meetings are also great motivators, and a professional-looking presentation can enhance any speech and increase its chances of making an impact (Chapter 14).
- *Multimedia.* Training is currently the single biggest use for multimedia technology, and sales training is an important candidate for this approach (Chapter 20).

Sales Force Management

- *Sales force automation.* Sales force automation software is dedicated to serving all the needs of salespeople. It can also be used to manage them more effectively (Chapter 10).
- *Time managers.* Time managers can help in scheduling and monitoring sales calls (Chapter 8).
- *Mapping software.* Mapping programs can be used to assign sales territories and plan sales visits (Chapter 11).

Sales Analysis and Forecasting

- *Spreadsheets.* Spreadsheets are essential in analyzing sales data and in creating forecasts of sales (Chapter 15).
- *Mapping software.* Mapping software can be used to detect trends in customer behavior based on geography (Chapter 11).

A day in the life of the modern marketing professional is likely to be long and hectic. These new technologies are available to reduce at least some of the burden.

Chapter Twenty-Four

The Value of Information

The Information Payoff

By now we have at least a gut feel that information and the associated technologies are often worth the expense, time, and effort they demand. But it helps to be a little more rigorous and specific than that.

Information payoffs can come in different forms. The following are some of them:

- *Cost displacement.* When an activity can be accomplished using less personnel time and/or fewer out-of-pocket expenses, there is a direct savings. This kind of productivity gain is probably the easiest kind of benefit to identify and measure.
- *Functional enhancement.* Doing more with the same resources also results in a productivity gain. A new telephone call distribution system, for example, that enables more customer calls to be handled by a given number of representatives provides a clear benefit. The *quality* of the marketing and sales functions can be improved in ways such as these.
- *Product/service enhancement.* Many products and services are enhanced by the use of technology. Securities trading via modem is an example. Other products are *enabled* by technology—they couldn't exist without it.
- *Better decisions.* By enabling you to amass and analyze larger amounts of data, better information and *intelligence* is available—about customers, suppliers, competitors, industry and

environmental trends, and so on. Ideally, this leads to better decisions, which in turn lead to better business results.

- *Offset competitor advantages.* Sometimes technology investments are made simply because the actions of competitors have made them a virtual necessity. "Technology changes the way you compete," and changes the way you *must* compete if a competitor has successfully introduced a technology innovation into the marketplace.

Communicating Value—IRR and NPV

Being able to understand the value of technology is typically not enough, unless you're paying for it yourself. You must be able to justify to your superiors or professional peers the often substantial costs involved, and to communicate the benefits you expect to result.

Every MBA learns a simple all-purpose method of cost-benefit analysis. It comes in two flavors, one called internal rate of return (IRR), the other called net present value (NPV). Both methods consider the effect of time on money. Put simply, a dollar received today is worth more than one received a year from now—the difference being the investment income that could have been earned in the intervening time.

Both methods gauge the value of an incremental stream of cash flows related to a project, acquisition, or other investment. Cash flows are both positive and negative—they include both funds expended and funds received as a direct result of undertaking the project. Cash flows for the economic life of the project should be included.

The math is essentially the same in each case, except that you're solving for a different variable. In an IRR analysis you're solving for the rate of return for the project, much like the rate of return on any investment. If it's above your *hurdle rate*—usually the rate you could get by doing something else with your money—you proceed with the project.

In an NPV analysis you're solving for the current value of expected future returns. If it's positive, the project is a money maker, and you go ahead.

The Value of Information

Measuring Technology Costs

Measuring outbound cash flows—here expenditures related to a technology project—seems relatively straightforward. What does the purchasing department say this hardware will cost? Right?

Only partially. Hardware expenditures reflect only about 15 percent of total lifetime outlays related to a microcomputer. The rest of the iceberg can include software, in-house and vendor support services, maintenance contracts, repairs, training, and fees paid to consultants for developing custom applications.

Sounds complicated. There is some good news, though. The people who evaluate technology expenditures in your company have probably factored these things into their evaluation process, so you may not have to reinvent that particular wheel.

Measuring Technology Benefits

Let's look at the return side of the equation. Positive incremental cash flows are a combination of *net cost reductions* and *revenue enhancements*. Cost reductions are based on the time and effort we'll save by working smarter through technology. These are usually pretty easy to evaluate.

Don't forget that savings may be a combination of *one-time* and *recurring* events. If we can eliminate a clerical position through technology, that money (salary and benefits) is saved year after year, hence we gain a recurring stream of positive cash flows.

Strictly speaking, any incremental savings should result in a real reduction in cash outflows. Too many cost-benefit analyses are based on planned savings that never actually materialize. And don't forget that word incremental. It means that you should only count savings that would not have been realized without the technology investment.

Revenue enhancements may be harder to get a handle on. Ironically, though, they often represent the key payoff for a marketing support technology. Here's where you literally use the machine to generate revenues for your company. It takes some creativity to evaluate these, but it can be done.

An Example

One good way of measuring increased revenues is to look at the *productivity of marketing activities*—output produced from a given level of input. Let's take an example from telemarketing. We can evaluate a desktop technology to help organize this function and make it more productive by increasing the number of calls that can be made within the time allotted (that is, with no increase or decrease in labor cost). The estimated payoff from using the new technology can be calculated like this:

> Calls made per person per year with the new technology
> − Calls made per person per year now
> = Incremental calls per person per year
> × Number of people making calls
> = Total incremental number of calls per year
> × The proportion of calls that result in new leads
> × The proportion of leads that result in new sales
> × The average net value of a new sale
> = The incremental cash flow per year

This positive cash flow is then analyzed with any other positive benefits (revenues or savings) and the costs of the investment, using either IRR or NPV. This is a somewhat simple-minded example, but it illustrates the point. Incidentally, it's also more rigorous than much of the technology justification done in the real world.

A Helpful Tool

The Information Edge, by N. Dean Meyer and Mary E. Boone (Dow Jones-Irwin, Homewood, IL, 1989), contains many examples of this kind of analysis drawn from real-world situations. Its basic thesis, like that of this book, is that desktop information technology can substantially change the way we do business and make us money, provided we subject it to the same analytic scrutiny we would any other investment decision. It includes chapters on systems planning and cost-benefit analysis that explain the concepts clearly, simply, and without resorting to either business school or computer jargon. It includes a good glossary of terms.

Each example is described both in words and in numbers. The examples are classified by category, with chapters on sales, marketing, operations, personnel, finance, product development, and business negotiations. The examples are from a variety of industries, and are well annotated.

The Value of Information

The marketing chapter includes sections illustrating the role of technology in:

- Formulating strategy
- Identifying prospects
- Timing sales efforts
- Creating a public image

One example shows how a $3,600 database search increased the likelihood that a law firm would win a lawsuit. This was estimated to have had a $900,000 impact on the outcome. This amounted to an internal rate of return of 25,000 percent.

Astounding payoffs like this really are possible. When presenting your information proposal to management, though, I recommend that you err on the side of being conservative in estimating the payoffs. In most cases you'll find that they still are staggering, and management will be a little less skeptical.

The Information Balance

Information is clearly a major business asset to be managed, with some companies spending generously on its generation and processing. In this section I'll argue that this spending often does not reflect the true competitive realities of the business, and I'll suggest ways to correct that.

A Test of Balance

Here's a test you can run on your business:

Step 1. Decide the mix between environmental (external to the company) and internal events that drive your business. Of all the factors that make it profitable, which of those are environmental (like general business conditions, moves by competitors, shifts in customer needs, etc.), and which are internal (like product costs, inventory levels, etc.)?

Step 2. Convert the result into a ratio. For example, if your answer in Step 1 was "About 60/40 environmental to internal," this converts to a ratio of 60 over 40, or 1.5.

Step 3. Determine your budget for managing internal information per year. This includes most of your MIS budget—that's usually a good proxy for the true figure. Be sure to include expenditures for hardware, software, and people. Let's say you're in a big company and this number is $1 million per year.

Step 4. Apply the ratio from Step 2 to the internal information budget from Step 3. In our illustration the result would be $1.5 million (1.5 times $1 million). This is a target figure for spending equivalence for environmental information.

Step 5. Obtain actual spending for environmental information—market research, competitive intelligence, industry studies, etc. This spending may be located in various places—marketing, planning, and/or the corporate library.

Step 6. From the result of Step 4 (target spending for environmental information), subtract the result of Step 5 (actual spending for environmental information.). The resulting figure is what I call the Environmental Information Deficit (EID) for your organization. If it's positive, you're spending too little on environmental information, or too much on internal information, relative to their importance to your business.

If you find mathematical representations more to the point, we can represent Steps 1 through 6 mathematically as follows:

$$EID = [D_e/D_i \times S_i] - S_e$$

where EID = Environmental Information Deficit

D_e = environmental factors driving the business

D_i = internal factors driving the business

S_i = spending on internal information

S_e = spending on environmental information

In many organizations the EID is positive, i.e., they underspend on information on the environment relative to its importance to their business.

What Does This Mean?

The enormous investment that many organizations have recently made in information technology has largely gone to measure internal events.

This is like flying a very complicated, expensive aircraft with very accurate instruments to measure fluid temperatures and pressures, rudder and aileron positions, etc.—but no with radar or air speed monitors.

Perfect information about internal workings clearly is no substitute for information about the business environment. For management to focus on the former, at the expense of the latter, is a serious omission, perhaps even a breach of its stewardship responsibilities.

I'm not suggesting that companies increase their total information spending. Most companies are still looking for ways to cut overhead costs. I *am* suggesting that information spending be reallocated to bring it into line with the business realities facing the company.

Nor am I suggesting that internal information is not useful in a marketing context. On the contrary, often there is lots of internal *data* produced, but not enough analytical attention is paid to it to make it useful, actionable *intelligence*.

Some types of companies, like professional services firms, have more of an imbalance between environmental and internal information than others, for example consumer goods companies. The latter more rigorously track their customers, their markets, and their competitors.

Why?

Why has this happened? Several forces have combined to create this situation, and understanding them may help us avoid or correct the problem.

- *Corporate culture.* Over the years, the delivery and use of corporate information has become almost completely tied to information technology, i.e., information systems. A massive effort, begun in the 1950s and continuing today, has been made to use these systems to manage internal information—financial accounting, timekeeping, billing, scheduling, etc. A whole new corporate culture has developed around the need to do this. Partly because of the technical nature of these systems, this culture is managed by technical specialists—not people who are experts in the business being managed.

    Here's a test. Ask your corporate MIS director "What's happening in the industry?" and chances are you'll get a readout of the latest developments in hardware and software—*not trends*

in the industry that the company as a whole is involved in. Management information has developed its own culture, apart from the industrial culture it serves.
- *The nature of information.* Much internal information, particularly that related to transactions or structured lists, is in a form that current technologies can handle effectively. Environmental information is often less structured, less regular in its production, and can come from a variety of sources. While technologies are evolving to handle unstructured information, they are much less developed than for structured information.
- *Our management models.* The original management information models, developed at Harvard Business School by Robert Anthony and others, emphasized the use of information as a control tool. The model's basic tenet: if you have information about a process, you can control that process. This model was developed in the relatively stable business environment of the late 1950s and early 1960s.

  Environmental information clearly does not fit into this model. Our need for it is not based on the fact that if we had it, we could control the environment. Our real goal is the *cost-effective reduction of risk and uncertainty.*

  Indeed, our business environment is much more dynamic than that of former decades. The management expert Tom Peters has described it as downright chaotic. This is not likely to change. We have deregulated many markets (transportation and telecommunications, for example), the value of our currency floats freely against others, and our capital markets are subject to greater volatility due to computer assisted trading. We need information, not to control these events, but to develop strategic responses to them decisively and quickly.
- *The tangible nature of information conduits.* Information *content* increasingly flows through information *conduits,* such as hardware and software. These conduits are like pipelines through which the content flows. The conduits are reassuringly tangible—the accountants like them because they have salvage value."

Information itself is the ultimate intangible. It is harder to value, and as a result sometimes is *devalued* relative to the more tangible conduits. *But it is information content, not conduits, that provides true strategic advantages.*

What Can We Do?

Many companies are at some level aware of this imbalance, and are taking steps to correct it. *PC Week* recently reported that top information executives see the following areas as top priorities for new systems spending:

- Sales
- Marketing
- Consumer contact
- Customer service

This is a positive sign, as each of these areas relates to the marketing and sales functions of the company.

How to Manufacture Intelligence

There is typically a mismatch between how information is produced and how it is used. Information is usually produced in a horizontal stream over time, i.e., as a chain of events about different topics. The stock ticker and real-time news feeds are living illustrations of this.

The typical use for information, though, is vertical—through time about a particular topic. In my consulting practice, I'm frequently called on to provide information about a particular topic (i.e., individual, company, industry, technology, etc.) over time.

The result—a timeline of sorts—enables you to see patterns and relationships that otherwise might go unnoticed. Trends become much more clear, and often you can begin to interpret a company's or business unit's strategy based on its actions.

Someday all this sorting of horizontal information into vertical slots will be done automatically by computers. Now most of it is still done manually.

Often you do not need to create new information through original research. You can access what has been created and published by others, i.e., journalists, managers, and consultants. There is often tremendous value in gathering, organizing, and analyzing this existing secondary information. Indeed, this creates a major line of business for companies such as FIND/SVP.

Here is a simple guide to how to use information effectively in the business world. It contains only four steps:

> **Step 1.** Access and retrieve from the *data universe* to form your *data environment*. Knowing where to look, and how to get what you need within your budget, are key challenges.
>
> **Step 2.** Organize and analyze your data environment to form *information*. Bringing together information from disparate sources will provide new insights.
>
> **Step 3.** Synthesize and communicate information to form *intelligence*, the basis for *decisions and actions*. You must sell the insights from Step 2 to key decision makers.
>
> **Step 4.** Monitor *business results* that ultimately result from that intelligence. This is the only true test of whether the decisions were better or not, after all.

You must execute all four steps to make information work for your company. Just as raw data is of little value if not analyzed, processed information is of little value if it is not woven into the actions and strategies of the organization.

Chapter Twenty-Five

The Future

Digital information technology, which began to be useful in business about 1950, has begun to evolve at what seems like an ever-accelerating pace, especially since 1980. In the first part of this chapter we'll look quickly at some new technologies that hold promise for marketers.

In the second part of this chapter, I've described several of the broad historical forces that are shaping the direction of information technology.

Emerging Technologies

The technologies described here have all begun to be introduced in commercial form. Although they have not, as yet, achieved widespread acceptance in the marketplace, each shows significant potential for applications in sales and marketing.

Alternative Input

Until recently, the vast majority of input to digital devices was done via keyboard. The QWERTY computer keyboard, of course, is a direct descendant of the typewriter keyboard. The arrangement of keys on that keyboard was designed in such a way that a good typist would not be able to go so quickly that the mechanical keys would jam. In other words, it was purposely designed to slow people down!

More important, many people who could benefit from computers can't type quickly. When many senior executives were coming through the ranks, they had secretaries who took dictation and did all the typing. There was a stigma attached to typing that translated into computer phobia.

Alternative input devices are substitutes for—or supplements to—the keyboard. Two forms seem ready for commercial success, voice recognition and pen-based technology.

Voice Recognition

Voice recognition technology translates spoken words into typed output. You talk clearly into a microphone, and the computer does what you say. This can range from interpreting software commands such as "Open a new document" to typing words as they are spoken. Commercial systems that plug into a regular PC cost about $5,000 and can be "trained" to recognize 30,000 different words. You train the machine to recognize a new word by typing the word, then speaking it several times. The instructions it recognizes include those to go back and correct mistakes.

Current systems can type about 50 words per minute—as much as a decent typist, but far slower than the 250 words per minute that an average person speaks. This gap will probably be closed in a few years.

Voice recognition has been implemented in medical settings, where, for example, input needs to be made to a patient's records while the doctor is doing other things with her or his hands. It is also being introduced into the legal community, where it can be used for transcribing depositions, trials, and other legal proceedings.

The main impact on marketing will be on executive information systems (EIS, see Chapter 22), which serve as real-time integration devices for the output of other systems.

Pen-based Technology

Pen-based technologies use an electronic stylus to input information to an electronic screen—sort of a high-tech version of an Etch-a-Sketch. The input is usually of the check-box variety, where the screen contains a simulated "form" for input. Experiments are also being conducted with handwriting recognition, though this seems like a very difficult problem.

Experts originally expected that pen technologies would be integrated into the next generation of personal digital assistants, those high-tech executive organizers like the Sharp Wizard. It is unclear now whether this will happen.

What seems more likely is that pen technology will be integrated into highly structured *vertical applications*, for very specific uses. Sales force call reports, for example, could be filled out much more quickly this way, and the results could be batched within the local device and transmitted daily to a central processing office.

Wireless

There is a major push on to free the PC user from the constraints of being plugged in. This was accelerated by the development of, in this order, laptops, notebooks, and subnotebook computers. All hardware components have been drastically reduced in size and weight. Efficiencies in power consumption have been developed, and extended-life battery technologies are beginning to appear.

Wireless technologies are an effort to make the communications aspects of PCs just as portable. Some early laptops contained *cellular modems,* which use cellular phone connections to hook into the regular telephone system for actual transmission of the information.

A more recent development is the *radio modem,* a device that uses existing radio signals to broadcast digital data. Two companies—RAM Mobile Data (a joint venture of BellSouth and RAM Broadcasting) and Ardis (a joint venture of Motorola and IBM)—have begun to build radio networks in the United States to carry these transmissions.

The RAM product links into many standard PC applications. By mid-1993, this service should be available in 100 U.S. cities.

The major impact here will be on electronic mail (see Chapter 12). The first benefit is that you will be able to get e-mail easily anywhere you go, without having to worry about plugging into hotel phone jacks and that sort of nonsense.

The other benefit—which could prove so significant that it will give e-mail the commercial push it has long needed—is that you won't have to call in to get your e-mail. E-mail will be directly transmitted to the receiving unit, much like a fax is directly transmitted to a fax machine. E-mail will become a much more elaborate version of the beepers we have now, which today carry only limited messages.

Portable Video

It will be very exciting for salespeople and marketers when the video revolution now hitting desktop machines becomes portable. It will mean that a salesperson can walk into a prospect carrying a self-contained, *interactive* presentation that includes animation and full-motion video (see Chapter 20).

Many of the prices of this technology are available today. A current desktop machine with a $500 attachment that sits under it (IBM makes one), can receive regular TV signals. Full-motion video can also be put onto a CD-ROM for playback on a PC (Chapter 20).

The screen technologies for portable machines is evolving quickly. The flat-screen color LCD screens are pretty good, and the next-generation *active matrix* screens are even better. (Unfortunately, they're very expensive, mainly due to the punitive import duties the United States imposes on screens made in Japan.)

When CD-ROMs become standardized, they will then be ready for mass-market acceptance. When the drives become small and light enough to be included in truly portable computers, we'll really have something. Sony has recently introduced a 2 1/2" read/write optical disk for use in its consumer-oriented Mini Disk music system, and technology like that could be a key component of portable video.

Virtual Reality

Virtual reality is a new technology in which images on a computer screen appear to be *dynamically* three-dimensional—you can simulate a "walk" around an object.

In some systems the images are manipulated *kinesthetically*, by moving one's body and limbs, and the "screens" are on the insides of goggles. These are the new *virtuality* systems that are beginning to appear in some high-tech video game arcades. Typically, two or more combatants roam a three-dimensional surface, alternately hiding from and taking "shots" at each other.

Virtual reality systems are already being used by some architects to demonstrate new designs before they are built. This technology has the advantage over drawings of being "three dimensional," and at the same time can be revised much more rapidly than a physical scale model.

Similarly, virtual reality is being used by graphic designers to mock up combinations of carpeting, upholstery fabrics, and window treatments.

Information Megatrends

To understand the future, one must first understand the present and the immediate past. Getting a grasp on the large forces that are driving the

The Future

information revolution can help us see where this revolution might lead next.

I call these large forces *information megatrends*. They fall into three categories:

- Trends in *hardware*
- Trends in *software*
- Trends in the *roles of information technology*

What follows are some concrete examples of how teach trend is being manifested.

Hardware Trends

Portability

Now that we've had a taste of portable information systems, it seems that we can't get enough. Many current developments have to do with enhancing the functionality of portable applications. These include:

- The development of wireless communications based on cellular telephone and FM radio
- The development of lighter, brighter, lower-cost flat-screen technologies
- The development of batteries that last longer than the current two- to three-hour average
- The development of *personal digital assistants* (PDAs) that are portable enough to go everywhere with you, and are "plugged in" at all times via wireless communications

Connectivity

One thing computers do very well is communicate. Their role in moving information has in many instances eclipsed their role in "computing" as such.

About 70 percent of PCs today are connected directly to other PCs through networks. Local area networks (LANs) tie into *wide area networks* (WANs), which in turn tie into *enterprise networks*. There are also public domain networks such as InterNet. These kinds of networks will eventually tie all computer users together, much as all telephone users eventually became able to connect with each other.

The demands on these connections will be strained by the need to transmit sound, graphics, and video information. The pipelines that tie these networks together are currently not sufficient to handle the job. Faster, broadband communications highways need to be built, based on fiber optic technologies and digital switches. Japan is already doing this. There is a proposal for a national data network—the National Research and Education Network (NREN)—that has languished so far, but that is likely to receive higher priority in the new administration.

Interoperability - Device Independence

Related to connectivity is the need for computers of different architecture types to be able to "talk" to each other. This is technically known as interoperability or *device independence.* Particularly since the introduction of Windows, a graphic operating environment for DOS machines, this has been happening among Macintosh and IBM-compatible computers, which together make up the overwhelming majority of desktop machines.

Many Windows applications run in identical form on the Macintosh, and create files that can be read by either version. This trend will continue due to the introduction of applications development tools that create a core code that is similar in both versions.

In the not-too-distant future, this will probably be a nonissue altogether. IBM and Apple are working on the PowerPC, a new breed of computer chip on which both of their operating environments will be based. They have also formed a joint venture (Taligent) to develop a new operating system for this new chip. This means that the two technologies are likely to merge, rather than having to accommodate each other.

Distributed Processing

Distributed processing is the migration of applications from large, centralized mini and mainframe computers to desktop PCs running on networks. Important, "mission-critical" applications continue to be migrated. I learned recently of a global, Fortune 100 pharmaceuticals company that migrated its accounting systems worldwide to a PC network. Some of the recent problems at IBM are due to their late recognition of this key trend.

As PC and network technologies continue to stabilize, the trend toward distributed processing will also continue. Mainframes will survive, but mainly as large *data reservoirs*. They will do less and less of the processing as such.

An analogy I like to make is that mainframe computers are like buses, where PCs are like cars. Buses are powerful and have lots of capacity—but they don't go exactly *where* you want to go exactly *when* you want to go.

Related to the spread of distributed processing is the *disintermediation* of many information activities, the reduction in the number of people who need to be involved in each piece of data processing and analysis work. With mainframes, everything had to be sent through *agents*—projects were submitted by users on punched cards or tape. The actual processing was done by someone who did that all day for other projects, but who had no actual understanding of the content of each project.

Disintermediation means that data processing is less of a stand-alone technical specialty, and more of a management discipline that supports other disciplines. It puts the information *consumer* that much closer to the production of the information. It won't be long—it's already starting to happen in some very sophisticated corporations—before the MIS function itself becomes decentralized, consisting at least partly of a network of representatives in each department that it supports.

Embedded Microprocessors

Stand-alone computers have set new benchmarks for flexibility. As the cost of hardware continues to drop, however, we're seeing more and more use of dedicated processing technology. This is processing technology that is optimized for doing only one thing best, and which does only that all day long. Supermarket UPC scanners are a good example, as are the microprocessors increasingly found in cameras and cars.

One of the most immediate and important manifestations of this phenomenon is the integration of the computer and the telephone. Several companies are already building phones with computers—including modems and small screens—inside them. Examples are the Citibank Enhanced Telephone and the AT&T SmartPhone.

Bigger, Better, Faster, Cheaper

The tendency of computer technology to accomplish bigger tasks, with higher quality, faster, and less expensively than could be done previously continues unabated. Within the past 10 years the amount of computing power you can buy has gone up significantly. The original IBM PC had

64 kilobytes of main memory. Released three years later, the original Macintosh had twice that. Today many of the newest machines have main memory capacities of 64 megabytes—1,000 times that of the original PC.

Likewise, it seems like only yesterday that the "advanced technology" IBM AT made a 50 percent leap in processor speed to 6 megahertz. Today, the latest thing is machines that run at 66 megahertz. All of this increased horsepower is available at roughly the same price points as yesterday's state-of-the art machines. Machines *equal* in power to the old machines are no longer available—but if they were, they would cost many times less than they originally did.

By "bigger," of course I'm referring to the size of the task accomplished, not the physical size of the machines, which are getting smaller, as noted. Computer scientists have a number of measures for task-efficiency—MIPS (millions of instructions per second), FLOPS (floating point operations,) Whetstones, Dhrystones, etc. The rest of us can think of this as basically the amount of work accomplished in a fixed unit of time.

Software Trends

Many of the hardware trends toward interoperability and "more for your money" also apply to software, in addition to other trends in software.

Better User Interfaces

The advent of graphic user interfaces (invented by Xerox, popularized by Apple, adopted by Microsoft) have led to a new level of user friendliness and convenience. While purists complain that these interfaces slow down the actual work of the computer, the fact is that the machines are so powerful today that this extra overhead is often not noticeable. Scientific studies have proved that people in general are more productive with graphic interfaces.

The design of the user interface has become so important that it has been the key issue in several copyright infringement lawsuits brought by software publishers, including a largely unsuccessful suit brought by Apple against Microsoft for use of the graphic interface in Windows.

A lot of attention is being paid to making software work the way we do. For example, several major software houses now sit their software engineers behind one-way glass to watch ordinary users work with new software. Fortunes are won and lost over the user interfaces and feature sets of new software.

Infoware

Infoware is loosely defined as a product that contains information content, in addition to the shell to manipulate the information. Some of the mailing list and phone directory products that have appeared recently are examples—they contain actual names, addresses, and phone numbers (see MarketPlace, profiled in Chapter 4). Many CD-ROM products will be of this kind.

Vertical Applications

Like embedded processors in the hardware arena, vertical applications are those that are optimized to do one limited set of things. Many marketing applications are of this type. For example, contact managers (see Chapter 9) are dedicated database programs. They are designed to be really good at contact list management—and in fact can't be used for anything else.

Trends in the Role of Information Technology

Computers in the Home

The experts agreed, "This technology will eventually be used by all businesses, but there's no good reason why anyone would need one at home." The technology being discussed was the telephone, and the prediction was made over 70 years ago.

The recent PC price wars have put many first-time computers into the home. All that's needed is one "killer application" to put this one over the top.

Computers in the Executive Suite

Like the telephone, the computer is making itself useful even to those who don't get their hands dirty. This will continue to happen as a result of two reinforcing trends: (1) the increasing usefulness of Executive Information Systems, and (2) the increasing computer literacy of the management ranks, particularly in the younger echelons.

Greater Role of Information in Strategy

Managers will become more and more accustomed to using information to make decisions, instead of relying on the best judgments of their assembled colleagues, as often happens now. The Japanese call this *management by fact* and tend to practice it much better than managers in the United States.

Accompanying this trend will be a change in the organizational structure of information management. This will mean, for example, a better integration of buyers/users of environmental information (like corporate libraries and market research and planning departments) and buyers/users of *internal* information (MIS departments). The attempt of some companies to create an officer-level position called a Chief Information Officer (CIO), responsible for overseeing both internal and environmental information, is a first manifestation of this trend.

Less Is More

The amount of information available is said to double roughly every four years. There are enormous amounts of information available and easily accessible, often leading to a condition I call *infoglut*. There's so much information, that we spend too much time digesting and analyzing it, and miss the very opportunities it represents!

Tools are beginning to appear to selectively *reduce* the amount of information we have to go through via intelligent filtering. We end up having a focused thread to guide us through this sea of information.

This has been an overview of new technologies and the trends that are driving technology development. There are, of course, large financial rewards available to those who develop successful new technologies. Consequently, there is much more competition than there used to be. Technology development has of necessity become more market driven than it was. Product development cycles are shorter and research is being used in more skillful ways to identify and evaluate market needs. We will all have fun watching—and becoming part of—this exciting time in the history of business.

Chapter Twenty-Six

Where Do We Go from Here?

Now we've seen all of the tools, and have some ideas about how to use them to develop new business, where do we go from here? As we approach a new century—and a new millennium—it's interesting to speculate on how this information revolution will affect us as marketers.

Confucius said, "Prognostication is dangerous, especially about the future." Sometimes even seeing where we are now is not obvious, and focusing on the present can give us clues as to the future.

We do at this point know some fundamental principles:

- *The U.S. economy is service driven.* More and more of our people work in "pure" service businesses, and more of our "product" companies have recognized the need for good service to support their products.
- *Information is an important business element.* Many of us are "knowledge workers." We work with information—words, numbers, and concepts.
- *Information is especially important in marketing.* If "sales" is defined as the movement of a good or service across the boundary between your organization and the customer's, then "marketing" is the movement of words, numbers, and concepts across that same boundary *in support of sales.* Marketing is like air support for the ground troops of the sales force—it makes their job easier, and often is the key difference between the success and failure of a sales effort. But in the end it is sales, not marketing, that brings money into our company.

- *We are in the middle of a great shift in information technologies.* "Middle" is a term used loosely; the shift began around 1950, and has only accelerated since then. Some have compared its impact as similar to the invention of movable type 500 years ago—an invention that changed forever the way business, and human life in general, is conducted.

Because sales/marketing is so tied in with the movement of information, any shift in information technologies would be expected to have a large impact on how sales/marketing operates. Consider the impact of television, which when introduced in 1950 had nowhere near the commercial impact that it has today.

Computers are on a curve following TV, and like the telephone before that. First they appeared only in companies, for industrial use. Then they began to appear in homes—but not everyone had one. Finally—and we're getting there fast—computers will be as ubiquitous as phones and TVs in people's homes. That story will be the next chapter in this unfolding drama.

Financial Markets—A Model

I believe that one good indication of where the future might take us comes from the financial markets. Wall Street invests more money in information—both conduits and content—than in any other segment of our economy. What are some of the features of the financial information landscape that may be replicated in other markets?

- *Real-time information.* Financial markets are known to react quickly to new information. It is, therefore, essential to get this information as quickly as possible. Buyers, sellers, and traders spend large sums of money to get information as soon as possible—in real time, to use the jargon.
- *Global information.* Downtown Manhattan as seen from the rooftop level looks like a garden of large mushrooms. The "mushrooms" are microwave antennas, designed to transmit and receive information globally in seconds. There is a whole business (arbitrage) built around identifying small price discrep-

ancies in global markets—discrepancies that when leveraged into huge trades add up to millions of dollars.
- *Heavy mix of environmental information.* A trading desk usually has a heavy flow of environmental information in real time. This information comes through terminals provided by the information providers—such as Reuters, Bloomberg, and Telerate. These companies provide financial information (prices and trading volumes), as well as general and business news, some of which may affect the pricing of securities.
- *Customer support systems.* Many firms, especially those that deal with retail accounts (for individuals), have elaborate customer support systems. Fidelity Investments, for example, has a networked desktop system that allows its reps—most of whom deal with customers by telephone, not in person—to call up detailed information about:
  - The customer—current holdings, trading history, investment preferences
  - The products—all of the mutual funds that the company sells
  - The company—where its branches are, what their operating hours are

  Some of these firms have begun to link their offices in various U.S. cities, in order to provide better service, and in order to facilitate the dissemination of leads that originate from a central point (such as a direct-response ad, for example).
- *Electronic linkages with customers.* Large institutional accounts like pension funds and insurance companies are often linked electronically to the people who manage their money. Now retail firms are beginning to provide scaled-down versions of these kinds of linkages to their individual clients. Charles Schwab and Fidelity Investments have both pioneered approaches to providing online trading and portfolio management to their clients.

Each of these trends in financial markets may be an advanced case of what could happen in the markets for, and marketing of, other goods and services. Granted that financial services represent the closest thing to a *purely* information-driven market there is—even physical stock certificates have all but disappeared. It therefore represents an extreme example of technology applications.

Nevertheless, each of the trends mentioned above—pioneered and refined in the financial services sector—has begun to appear in other sectors as well, such as consumer packaged goods. I think we can count on the further evolution of these trends in this direction.

What We'd Like to Know

Someone has defined marketing as "serving customer needs at a profit." Certainly the sea change in marketing over the last 20 years is toward an approach that is more market driven than it used to be. Whereas the role of marketing used to be to get the things being manufactured by the company moved off the shelves, now that role includes *making sure those things on the shelves are the right things.*

Doing this involves obtaining the right mix of business intelligence elements from the business environment. In the ideal world, as sales and marketing people we would know about the following environmental forces:

- *The general business environment*
    - How are general business conditions trending?
    - What will happen to interest rates and capital availability?
    - What's happening with overall capital spending and manufacturing capacity?
    - Where is consumer confidence headed?

- *Our market*
    - What is its size, by segments?
    - What are the growth trends?
    - Who are the major players?
    - What are their market shares?
    - What new developments have occurred?
    - What is likely to happen in the future?
    - What opportunities are there?

- *Our customers and prospects*
    - What do they want from our products and services?
    - What do they like now?
    - What do they think could be better?
    - Who are the decision makers?
    - What are they like?
    - How are decisions made?
    - What is going on internally that may affect their relationship with us?

- *Our competitors*
    - What is their strategic direction?
    - What new products are they introducing?
    - What kinds of promotions and advertising are they doing?
    - How well are they doing?
    - Who are their major customers?
    - How large is their sales force?
    - How is it organized and compensated?

- *Other companies not our competitors*
    - Has this approach we're considering ever been tried in another industry?
    - What happened?
    - Would it work for us?
    - What are the most effective practices in this area?

- *Ourselves* Internal information is sometimes ignored in a marketing context, but it can be very useful.
    - How well are our products and services performing?
    - Are we providing the product/service mix and product/service features the market wants?
    - Is our quality what it should be?
    - Did we ever try this before?
    - What happened?

Note that in companies that do get all of this information, much of the time it comes from different activities undertaken by different functions in different parts of the company. The following table illustrates the various activities that serve as sources for this important marketing/sales information.

Information About	Source Activity/Function
General business environment	Strategic planning; Economics
Market	Market research
Customers and prospects	Sales
Competitors	Competitive intelligence
Other companies	Benchmarking
Ourselves	Management information systems

All too often there is no single organizational point of integration that brings this information together. The result is reduced efficiency and effectiveness of the information management function overall, due to:

- *Overlaps and duplication.* Two different functions may be gathering and analyzing the same information.
- *Gaps.* The lack of overall cohesion in the effort leaves some key elements uncovered.
- *Missed synergies.* Information often becomes more valuable when matched with other information. When information stays in functional pockets, this does not happen.
- *Failures to communicate.* This is probably the single biggest pitfall in the information profession—the failure to get the right information to the right person at the right time.

The "information wish list" described in the preceding pages is incomplete without these qualifications:

- *The information must be timely.*
- *The information must be easy to access.* Formats must be attractive, informative, and concise.
- *The information must be manipulable.* Information that can be pushed, "what-ifed," compared to other data, and so on, takes on another level of value from static information.

The Information Paradox

Business information in most companies lies on a series of organizational islands—creating what Professor Warren McFarlan of Harvard calls the "information archipelago." This has created a fundamental paradox:

- *Information is a corporate asset.* People don't generally buy research reports or information technology out of their own pockets.
- *Information is the corporate asset most easily dispersed.* Information can be transmitted at the speed of light to practically anywhere on the globe.
- *Yet—information often stays in localized pockets.* Granted, there may be political reasons why this happens. Knowledge is power, and shared knowledge is shared power.

But aside from these intentional barriers, there are lots of unintentional barriers created by the fact that we still use many of our advanced tools in primitive ways.

The point is that to solve this paradox there doesn't need to be an *organizational* focal point for all of the information a company has. It can be a *virtual focal point*—a point that exists not in one department or one physical location, but in the electronic connections that increasingly define what organizations are.

This basic paradox can be solved by building an *organizational knowledge base* that contains inputs from all of the information sources listed above. Network technology gives us the ability to transcend organizational boundaries. By sharing knowledge, we share power—and this makes us *all* more powerful.

Reprise: The Marketing Machine

Back to our original theme. By now I hope it's clear that I've used the term "marketing machine" in two ways:

- *Literally.* The marketing and sales supports that use computers as their base.
- *Figuratively.* An organized, systematic approach to the many routine, tedious parts of marketing.

The literal marketing machine is a tool that enables the figurative marketing machine to be realized. The computer becomes a platform—a command center, if you like—for the organization of the *soft machine* of marketing and sales activities.

The computer will enable us to link internally to become a stronger organization. It will enable us to link directly with our customers, to make the boundaries between "us and them" seem less significant.

Computer-Assisted Sales and Marketing (CASM)

What we've described in the book is a series of tools that, when taken together, form a powerful suite of applications for sales and marketing. The applications, as yet, are basically separate, and it's still up to the user to set them up and make them work together.

These are likely to become more integrated over time. Two of the newer classes of software described here, Sales Force Automation and Scanner Data Analysis, contain elements of some of the other, stand-alone packages (word processing, e-mail, and spreadsheets, for example).

Interestingly, the same thing has happened with software support for manufacturing. In its early stages, this amounted to separate applications (mostly on minicomputers) for product design, materials planning and handling, job scheduling, and other manufacturing functions.

During the 1980s this patchwork approach to manufacturing applications evolved into Computer Integrated Manufacturing (CIM), which included and superseded many of the stand-alone functions that preceded it.

The same may happen for sales and marketing applications, whose life cycle is behind that for manufacturing applications (and *way* behind that for financial applications). This all may evolve into something that by analogy I'll call Computer-Assisted Sales and Marketing (CASM).

How would such a system look? Let's go back to our manufacturing analogy. Computer Integrated Manufacturing systems are built around the flow of *materials* through the manufacturing process—from purchasing, to receiving, to raw materials, to subassemblies, to finished goods, to final sale. *Materials* form the unifying element for the manufacturing process, and the systems model the process.

What is the unifying element for the sales and marketing process? There are two choices that logically occur:

- *The product/service.* Consumer products move out into wholesale distribution channels, then into retailers, then finally into the hands of end purchasers. Industrial products go through sales reps or distributors, then to business users. Services tend to move more directly to end users, whether they are businesses or individual consumers.
- *The customer.* The buyer of the product or service. Where there is a relationship being built and maintained, this is a more logical choice. A system could track a potential customer through the various stages of purchase: awareness, evaluation, purchase, customer support, repeat purchase.

There's a lot of evidence to support the hypothesis that the "market-driven" philosophy espoused by many companies in the 1980s has actually had some results. Consumer service companies have undertaken a series of moves designed to built repeat purchases—including the airlines (frequent flier miles) and the credit card companies (purchase discounts and credits).

Even consumer goods companies have realized that they have—or could have—relationships of a sort with their customers. Brand loyalty is seen less as a mass phenomenon, and more as the sum of many individual transactions.

Some consumer goods companies are even building databases of their users—people whom they can call on to come to focus groups or answer phone interviews. Ironically, one way they sometimes gather names for these user databases is from customer complaint calls. Customers who are vocal about their opinions—whether positive or negative—can be a great source of direct feedback about a product or an advertising or promotional campaign.

I'll hedge on this one by saying that both the customer and the service/product need to be tracked—in that order. Many banks, for example, are building Customer Information Files (CIF) that give total account information for a particular individual across all the bank's services. This approach, pioneered by Fidelity Investments, allows banks to cross sell other services to customers who may need them.

The banks' older systems tracked each product/service line separately. There was little cross linking, and therefore each business unit was essentially ignorant of the clients of the other units—each of whom would have been a key prospect for the bank's other services.

People are the ultimate buyers, even of industrial goods and services. People should be at the center of the Computer Assisted Sales and Marketing solar system.

INDEX

A

Access, 147
Account(s), 70, 71, 129
  see National
  applications, 174
  management, 17, 103
  representatives, 79
Accounting
  records, 18
  software, 5
AccuZip6, 37
ACT!, 72-74, 87
Action, 157
Active matrix screen, 200
Ad(s), 42-43
Add-in functions, 24, 25-26
Advertising, 17, 181
  copy, writing, 26
  storyboard, 156
Alarm, 65, 66
Aldus Pagemaker, 9
Alternative input, 197-199
America OnLine, 96, 122, 133
American Business Information/Lists, 37, 38
American Business Research Network, 172-173
Analysis, 35
  see Competitive, Customer, Data, Financial, Product, Profitability, Sales, Scanner, Spatial, Survey
Annual sales, 36
Apple, 202, 204
  Computer, 10
  Macintosh, 9

Applications, 5, 28, 142
  see Account, Computer, Credit, Inbound, Inter-organizational, Marketing, Outbound, Paradox, Personal, Sales, Software, Vertical, Word processing
  generator, 143
  maintenance, 14
Archiving, 92
Area-related data, 83
Artificial intelligence, 175
Asynchronous, 48
Atlas
  files, 87
  GIS, 86
  software, 88
Auto-attendant feature, 56
Automation, see Sales force, Work flow

B

Back order, 16
Background operation, 56
Banners, 136
BBS, *see* Bulletin board system
BellSouth, 199
BigmOuth, 59-60
Body text, 23
Borland International, 7, 92
Boundaries, *see* Geographic, Hierarchical, Organizational
Brand manager, 149
Broadcast fax, 48
Brochures, 42
Budget, 28
  see Public relations

Budgeting, 115-116
Built-in
  reports, 73
  statistics, 139
Bulletin board system (BBS), *see* Electronic
Bulletproofing, 117
Business
  computers, 15
  data, 85
  development, 3, 14
  enterprise, 5
  management support, 17
  marketing plans, 174
  professional, 5
  proposals, 26, 145, 174
  tracking, 115
Business-to-business
  marketing, 36
  research, 136

C

Cable television, 31
Calculating software, 141
Calendaring, 100
Call reports, 16
Campaign management, 35-36
Career opportunities, 43
Cash flow, 13, 188-190
CASM, *see* Computer-assisted
CAT IV, 74
Catalogs, 43
CATI, *see* Computer-Assisted Telephone Interviewing
CD, *see* Photo
CD-ROM, 36, 37, 77, 86, 126, 153-155, 183, 200, 205
Cellular modem, 199
Channel support, 184
Character recognition
  see Optical
  software, 47
Charitable organization, 4
CIF, *see* Customer information file
Clip art, 109

library, 40, 44
Clippings tracking system, 145
Collateral inventory system, 144-145
Color
  see Multiple-color
  separation, 39
Communications
  see Corporate, Sales force
  software, 5, 92
Compatibility, 51, 146-147
  see Network
Compensation, 43
Competitive
  analysis, 85, 181
  intelligence, 150-151
Competitor(s), 211
Complete Answering Machine, The, 60
CompuServe, 122, 128, 131-132, 171
Computer
  see Apple, Business, Desktop, Laptop, Mainframe, Microcomputer, Minicomputer
  applications, *see* Work group
  magazines, 8
  operations, 5
  technology, 13
Computer-Assisted
  sales and marketing (CASM), 214-216
  Telephone Interviewing (CATI), 16, 135
ComputerVision, 116
Concatenated variables, 140
Conduit, 208
  see Information
Conferencing, 100, 101
Connectivity, 201
Consultant, 17-18, 71
  see Independent
Consumer
  contact, 195
  databases, 121, 122
    marketing/sales applications, 126-127
  needs, 31

Index

research, 128
Contact list, 143
Contact management, 182
   software
      benefits, 70
      case study, 70-71
      description, 69
Contact management system, *see* LAN-based
Contact managers, 65, 69-74, 181, 183
   integration ease, 71-72
   marketing/sales applications, 70
   selection, 71-72
   speed, 71
Contact
   identification, 125
   software, 72
Control palette, 45
Copying, 92
Corporate
   communications, 100, 101-102
   culture, 193-194
   managers, 13
   role model, 13
   technology manager, 15
   training, 153
Cost control, 33
Cost displacement, 124, 187
Credit applications, 174
Crop marks, 42
Cross-selling, 71
   information, 17
Cross-tabulation, 135
   see Tabulation
CSC Index Group, 81
Customer, 211
   activity, 17
   analysis, 17
   communications, 18, 172
   complaint tracking, 17
   contact, 34
   database, 33
   education, 18
   information, 16
      file (CIF), 33, 215
   list, 32
   newsletters, 43
   profitability, 17
   satisfaction, 18, 137
   segmentation analysis, 143
   service, 17, 81, 100, 127, 175, 195
   support, 184
   system, 18, 209
Cutting/pasting, 24

D

Data, 12
   see Area-related, Business, Database, Demographic, Digital, Electronic, Mainframe, Point-oriented, Scanner, Survey, Test-market
   access, 117
   analysis, 16, 135
   attributes, 83
   collection, 135
   Desk, 87
   elements, 84
   entry, 136, 143
      see Proprietary
   file, 24
   items, 72
   management program, 85
   modem, 47
   One, 81
   presentation, 115
   reservoirs, 203
   table, 142
   tracking, 80
Database(s), 66, 83, 113, 141
   see Consumer, Customer, Electronic, Fourth, Flat file, Merged, Online, Professional, Proposal, Public, Relational
   developer, 6
   environment, 104
   files, 121
   management program, 27
   management software, 70
      description, 141-142
   manager, 141-147, 181, 182

case studies, 144-146
marketing/sales applications, 142-143
marketing, 17, 35, 174
publishing, 146
searching, 143
software, selection, 146-147
system, 121, 142
Data-based mapping, 84
Data-parse formats, 117
DayMaker, 65-67, 72
views, 66
DayRunner, 64
Day-Timer, 64
Dbase, 163
DEC VAX, 87
Decision support, 17
Dedicated software, 70
Delivery
dates, 16
system, 17
Dell, 10
Demand forecasting, 17
Demographic
data, 85
files, 33
information, 71
Desktop
computer, *see* Stand-alone
geographic information systems, 84
platforms, 135
printer, 40
Desktop publishing, 39-46, 180-182, 184
advanced features, 44
benefits, 41-42
case study, 43-44
compatibility, 44
control, 41-42
cost, 41
description, 39-41
DTP, 39-44
see Work-group
ease, 44
marketing/sales applications, 42-43
quality, 41

selection, 44
Device independence, 202
Dialing codes, 72
Dialog, 122, 129-131, 132
files, 130
Digital data, 56
Direct mail, 31, 84, 181-182
creation, 26
pieces, 42
quality improvement, 33
retailers, 7
Direct mailing, 24
Direct marketing, 48-49, 181-182
Direct response, 49
Directories, 96
Disintermediation, 203
Distributed processing, 202-203
Distribution, 17
channel communications/support, 172
planning, 84
Document assembly, 173-175, 183-184
Document assembly software
benefits, 174
description, 173-174
marketing/sales applications, 174
DOS, 7, 9, 40, 104, 123, 202
software, 10
user, 4
Dow Jones News/Retrieval, 97, 122, 132
Drexel Burnham Lambert, 32
Drill down, 167, 169
DTP, *see* Desktop publishing
Dun & Bradstreet, 36, 125

E

EDI, *see* Electronic
Editing, 24
EID, *see* Environmental
EIS, *see* Executive
Electronic
catalogs, 78
conferencing, 171
data interchange (EDI), 17, 50, 78, 176
database, 168

Index

documents, 168
filing, 24
linkages, 209
mapping, 16
network, 100
organizers, 63
searcher, 130
Electronic bulletin board, 121, 183, 184
   software
      benefits, 172
      description, 171
      marketing/sales applications, 172
   system, 96
Electronic mail (E-mail), 48, 91-98, 100, 101, 104, 131, 168, 171, 180, 199
   benefits, 93-94
   case study, 95
   description, 91-93
   fax comparison, 93-94
   features, 92-93
   marketing/sales applications, 95
   physical mail comparison, 94
   system, selection, 95-96
   voice mail, 94
E-mail, *see* Electronic mail
Embedded microprocessors, 203
Emerging technology, 197-200
Employees, 43
   number, 36
End users, 14, 92
Enterprise network(s), 201
Entrepreneurs, 3
Enveloping, 51
Environmental
   awareness, 124
   information deficit (EID), 192
Envoy Systems, 81
Excel, *see* Microsoft
Executive information system (EIS), 149, 150, 198, 205
   software
      benefits, 170
      description, 169-170
      marketing/sales applications, 170
Expert systems, 184

Export, *see* Software

F

Fax, 47-54, 70, 92, 180, 182
   see Broadcast, LAN-based, PC-based
   back systems, 53
   case study, 50
   electronic mail comparison, 93-94
   Manager, 51-52
   marketing/sales applications, 48-50
   modem, 47, 48
   server, 51
   software, 92
      benefits, 48
      description, 47
      selection, 51
Fax-back, 49
   capabilities, 171
Fax-on-demand, 49
Federal Communications Commission, 49, 58
Field, 141
   see Pop-up, User-defined
   office communications, 17
   sales, 80
File(s), 123
   see Customer, Demographic, Dialog, Index, Procedural, Report, Screen
   backup, 5
   downloading, 171
   management, 11
   functions, 24
Filemaker Pro, 147
Filing, *see* Electronic
Financial
   analysis routines, 113
   information, 131
   management software, 5
   markets, 208-210
FlashFax, 53
Flat-file database, 141
Flexibility, 15, 64, 72, 138
   see Template
Focus groups, 137-138
Folio Views, 169

Follow-up, 64
 letters, 26
Food manufacturers, 31
Footers, *see* Headers/footers
Forecasting, 115
Forest & Trees, 171
Forum(s), 123, 131
Forward, *see* Store and forward
Forwarding, 56
Fourth Dimension, 147
 database, 85, 87
FrameMaker, 45
Franklin, 64
Front end, *see* Integrated
Front-end software, 149
Full-text information, 129
Functional enhancement, 187
Fundraisers, 4

G

Gantt chart, 162
 program, 85
Gateway 2000, 10
General business environment, 210
Genigraphics, 111
Geographic
 boundaries, 102
 breakdown, 32
 information systems (GIS), 83
  see Desktop
 map, 83
 specificity, 86
Geographical area, 36
GeoQuery, 73, 87-88
GIS, *see* Geographic information systems
Global information, 208-209
GoldMine, 71
Grammar checkers, 25-26, 29
Graphic user interface (GUI), 9, 29, 204
 advantages/disadvantages, 9-10
Graphics, 29, 39, 45, 48, 107-110, 116, 123, 154
 handling, 51
 Link, 111
Group
 addressing, 92
 edits, 73
Groupware, 91, 99-106, 182
 benefits, 101-102
 case studies, 102-103
 description, 100
 hardware integration, 104
 marketing/sales applications, 100-101
 selection, 104
 software integration, 104
GUI, *see* Graphic user interface

H

Hand-outs, creation, 26
Hard copy, 107, 108
Hard disk, 168
 maintenance, 5
Hard-copy, 93, 95
 management report, 102
 output, 111
 system integration, 65
Hardware, 116
 see Groupware, Telecommunications
 cards, 11
 expenditures, 189
 technology, 80
 trends, 201-204
Headers/footers, 23
Hierarchical boundaries, 102
Home entertainment/education, 153
Horizontal information, 195
Hurdle rate, 188
Hypercard, 156, 167
Hypertext, 167

I

IBM, 75, 118, 162, 199, 200, 202-204
 mainframe, 87
IBM compatibles, 9, 11, 72, 97, 114, 123, 130, 143, 154, 156, 162
 advantages, 10
Icons, *see* User-definable
IdeaBank, 165
IdeaFisher, 167
Identification code, 56, 92

Index

Image recorder, 111
Inbound
 applications, 18-19
 telemarketing support, 57-58
Independent consultants, 3
Independents, 3
Index files, 142
Information, 12, 115, 123, 125, 126, 145, 193, 195
 see Customer, Demographic, Desktop, Environmental, Executive, Financial, Full-text, Global, Horizontal, Internal, Management, Marketing, Personal, Pricing, Real-time, Structured, Unstructured
 balance, 191-195
 component, 127
 conduit, 194-195
 consumers, 14
 content, 194, 195
 conveyance, 57
 Edge, 190
 Lens, 94
 manufacturing, 195-196
 megatrends, 200-206
 nature, 194
 paradox, 213
 payoff, 187-191
 sharing, 100
 technology, 3, 4, 15, 18
 trends, 205-206
 value, 187-196
Infoware, 33, 205
Input, *see* Alternative
Installed base, 10
Integrated
 front end, 138
 OCR, 51
Integration, *see* Contact manager, Groupware, Hard-copy, Mapping package
Intelligence, 12, 124, 187, 193
 see Competitive, Market
Interactive, 155
 presentation, 199
 sales presentation, 78
Interface, 138, 143
 see User
Internal
 information, 206, 211
 MIS department, 32
 rate of return (IRR), 188, 190
Interoperability, 11, 202
Inter-organizational
 application, 101
 network, 101
Intra-organizational network, 101
Inventory management, 17
Investment, 4
Invoice status, 16
IRR, *see* Internal

J

Justification, 23, 29

K

Kerning, 39, 44
Keyword search, 167
Knowledge Index, 130
Kodak, 41

L

LabelSet, 139
LAN, *see* Local area network
LAN-based
 contact management system, 71
 see Local area network
 fax server, 50
Landscape mode, 107
Language, *see* Macro, Paradox, Scripting
Laptop computers, 5, 11, 14, 71, 75, 116
Leads management, 183
Learn mode, 96
Lexis, *see* Nexis
Life cycle, 17
Linkage, 96
Linotronic, 40
List

224   Index

see Contact, Customer, Mailing, Summary
counts, 36
management functions, 32-33
management software package, 37
sorting, 36
source integration, 34
Local area network (LAN), 51, 99, 172, 201
see LAN-based
Logistics, 17
Lotus Development, 7, 97
 1-2-3, 9, 101, 105, 118, 143, 163
 Express, 97, 98
 Notes, 101-105

M

Macintosh, 7, 29, 40, 45, 64, 72, 75, 85, 87, 104, 111, 117, 118, 123, 138, 154, 156, 161, 167, 202, 204
see Apple
 advantages, 10-11
 user, 4
Macro
 function, 73
 language, 113
Macromind Director, 157
Mail
see Direct, Electronic, Voice mail
 merge, 24, 27
 survey, 137
Mailbox, see Voice
Mailer(s), 42-43, 155
Mailing, targeting, 34
Mailing list, 31, 143
 management, 32
  software, description, 32-33
  software, marketing/sales applications, 33-34
 managers, 27, 31-38, 181, 182
  benefits, 33
  selection, 34-36
Mainframe, 202, 203
see IBM
 computers, 32, 55, 75, 79, 83

data, 146
Management
see Account, Business, Campaign, Contact, Data, Database, File, Financial, Hard copy, Inventory, Leads, List, Project, Quality, Response, Sales, Sales force
 model, 194
Management Information System (MIS), 13, 203
see Internal
 MIS budget, 191
 MIS director, 193
 MIS departments, 14, 32, 206
 MIS managers, 4
Manager, 3
see Brand, Contact, Corporate, Database, Mailing list, Marketing, MIS, Personal, Project, Sales force, Time
Mapping
see Data-based, Electronic, Street-based, Thematic
 package
  integration, 86
  selection, 86
Mapping software, 83-90, 184, 185
 benefits, 84
 case studies, 85-86
 description, 83-84
 marketing/sales applications, 84-85
Margin(s), 23
Market, 210
see Financial
 fragmentation, 31
 intelligence system, 17
 research, 180-181
 scoping, 125
Marketers, see Nonprofit
Marketing, 12, 81, 180-182, 195
see Business-to-business, Computer-assisted, Database, Niche/regional, Relationship, Sales force, Target, Telemarketing
 activities, productivity, 189

Index

applications, 6
   see Marketing/sales applications
development, 3, 14
information system, 16
Information Systems, 81
intelligence, 16
machine, 13-19, 213-216
managers, 14, 18
problems, 5
professionals, 3
research, 16
support, 17
Marketing/sales applications
   see Consumer, Contact manager, Database manager, Desktop, Document, Electronic bulletin, Executive, Fax, Groupware, Mailing list, Mapping, Multimedia, Presentation, Professional, Project, Sales force, Scanner, Spreadsheet, Survey, Text, Thought, Time management, Timekeeping, Voice mail, Word processing
MarketPlace Business, 36-37
Marking, 35
Mastering, 155
Maximizer, 74
MCI Mail, 95, 97
Media
   see Multimedia
planning, 85
selection, 17
Memory, 11
   see Organizational, Read Access
management, 11
Menu-driven, 123
software, 79
Merge and purge, 32, 34
Merged database, 71
Message
   answering/forwarding, 92
   encryption, 104
   filtering, 94
   scanning, 92
   targeting, 33

Microcomputer technology, 14
Microphone, 97
Microphone II, 98
Microsoft, 7, 73, 92, 204
   Excel, 73, 116, 117-118
   Project, 164
   Word, 29-30, 73
Minicomputers, 32, 55, 83
MIS, see Internal, Management Information System
Modem, 92, 96, 172
   see Cellular, Data, Fax, Radio
Motorola, 199
MPC, see Multimedia
Multimedia, 11, 109, 153-157, 181, 183, 184
   case study, 156-157
   marketing/sales applications, 155-156
   PC (MPC) Marketing Council, 154
   software, description, 153-155
Multiple responses, 139
Multiple-color printing, 39

N

National
   accounts strategy, 43
   Research and Education Network (NREN), 202
Net cost reductions, 189
Net present value (NPV), 188, 190
Network, 40, 66
   see Electronic, Enterprise, Inter-organizational, Intra-organizational, Local area, Personal, Wide area
compatibility, 51
Networking, 11
Network-readiness, 146
Newsletter, see Customer
Nexis/Lexis, 122, 132
Niche/regional marketing, 17
Nickelodeon, 128
Nielsen, A.C., 149
   Workstation, 151-152
Nonprofit
   marketers, 4

organization, 4
Nonrecurring sales, 42
Notebook computers, 5, 75
   see Sub-notebook
NovaLink Pro, 173
NPV, see Net
NREN, see National

O

OCR, see Integrated, Optical
Off-line composition, 93
OneSearch, 129
On Time, 67
One-time event, 189
Online
   advertising, 127
   search, 168
   shopping, 126
   sources, 125-126
   systems, 128
      benefits, 123-124
Online databases, 121-133, 141, 181-183
   case studies, 127-128
   content, 128
   description, 121-123
   ease, 128
   pricing, 128
   selection, 128
Online systems, 171
Optical
   character recognition (OCR), 52
      see Integrated
   software, 51, 92
   disk, 168
Order(s)
   entry/processing, 172
   taking, 57
Organization
   see Charitable, Nonprofit
   tools, 5
Organizational
   boundaries, 102
   knowledge base, 213
   memory, 102
OS/2, 7, 9, 71, 104, 143

Outbound
   applications, 18-19
   telemarketing support, 57-58
Outline, 110
Outliners, 25
Outlining, 167
   program, 29
Output quality, 146
Overhead transparencies, 26
Ownership type, 36

P

Page layout, 26, 44
PageMaker, 44-45
PAL, see Paradox
Palette, see Control
Pantone, 45
Paradox, 143-144, 147
   Application Language (PAL), 143
Pasting, see Cutting/pasting
PBC, see Pen-based computing
PBX phone system, 55
PC, see Personal computer
PDA, see Personal digital
PDE, see Proprietary
Pen technology, 78
Pen-based
   computing (PBC), 78
   technology, 198-199
Personal computers, 3, 5, 14, 18, 39, 63, 75, 136
   PC, 11, 32, 35, 38, 45, 48, 55, 57, 59-60, 92, 94, 114, 123-125, 128, 136, 162, 174, 198, 199, 200, 203, 205
      see Multimedia
   network, 170
PC application, 48
PC Board, 173
PC games, 43
PC-based fax, 93
PC-based systems, 55
PC users, 143
Personal digital assistant, 201
Personal information manager, 63

Index

Personnel, 78
   scheduling, 13
Persuasion, 112
Phone dialers, 69
Photo CD, 41
Physical mail, electronic mail comparison, 94
Planner, *see* Software
Planning, 115-116, 160
Point-of-sale, 16
   systems, 17
Point-oriented data, 83
Political
   campaigns, 4
   polling, 127-128
Pop-up field, 72
Portability, 201
Portable video, 199-200
Postal Service, 32
Potential value, 3
Power conservation, 5
PowerBook, 11
PowerPC, 202
PowerPlay, 170, 171
PowerPoint, 110-112
Presentation
   see Data, Sales
   package, 150
Presentation software, 40, 107-112, 139, 183, 184
   benefits, 109
   description, 107-109
   ease, 110
   marketing/sales applications, 110
   selection, 110
Press inquiry tracking, 100
Price, 10
Pricing, 16, 115
   information, 101
   strategies, 17
Primary research survey, 127
Prime Computer, 116
Printer, *see* Desktop
Procedural files, 142
Procomm, 97, 98

Prodigy, 96, 122, 123, 132
Product, 12
   analysis, 17
   distribution, 127
   mix analysis, 17
   reports, 17
   specifications, 16
   strategy, 17
Productivity, 15
Product/service enhancements, 18, 187
Professional databases, 121, 122
   marketing/sales applications, 124-126
Professional Mail, 37
Profitability, 16
   see Customer
   analysis, 17, 115
Progressive disclosure, 112
Project, *see* Microsoft
Project management, 64, 66, 100
   software
      benefits, 160
      description, 159-160
      marketing/sales software, 161
      selection, 161
Project managers, 159-164, 181
Project reports, 139
Projectors, 107, 108
Promotion(s), 16, 17, 34, 101
Promotional strategy, 17
Proposal(s), 42
   see Business
   database, 145-146
   kit, 27-28
Proprietary data entry (PDE), 139
Prospects, 211
   identification, 191
Prospecting, 34
   systems, 17
Protocol, 91
   see Telecommunications
Public
   databases, 91
   image, 191
   relations budget, 17
   Relations Manager, 85, 86

sector, 4
Publishing, *see* Desktop
Purge, *see* Merge and Purge

Q

Q & A, 147
QBank, 165
Quality management, 101
Quark XPress, 45
Quattro Pro, 118
Query
   by example, 143
   table, 142
Query-building, ease, 146
QuickTime, 156

R

Radio modem, 199
RAM
   see Random Access Memory
Broadcasting, 199
Random Access Memory
   RAM, 11
Random sampling, 36
Realignment, 84
Real-time information, 208
Record, 34, 35, 139
Record-keeping software, 141
Recovery tools, 5
Recurring event, 189
Re-engineering, 19
Relational database, 141
Relationship
   building, 183
   marketing, 64
Report, 144
   see Built-in, Hard copy, Project, Summary
   files, 142
Reporting options, 80
Response
   management system, 144
   systems, 137
Retailer, *see* Direct mail
Risk

reduction, 194
tolerance, 69
Rolodex, 67, 69
Runtime, 142

S

SABRE, 131
Sales, 12, 16, 183-184, 195
   see Annual, Computer-assisted, Field, Nonrecurring
   analysis, 185
   applications, 6
      see Marketing/sales applications
   development, 3
   effort, timing, 191
   forecasting, 16, 185
   management, 81
   performance analysis, 16
   presentations, 110, 155
   professionals, 3
   promotions, 17
   prospecting, 85
   reporting system, 43
   resources, 43
   support, 16, 17, 80, 184-185, 207
   system, 17
   territory management, 84
   training, 155, 185
Sales Automation Association, 76
Sales force
   automation (SFA), 75-82, 172, 183, 184
      benefits, 76
      commitment, 80-81
      case studies, 78-80
   communications, 110
   coordination, 58
   management, 16, 17, 101, 161
   managers, 91
   software
      description, 75-76
      marketing/sales applications, 76-78
   support, 75
Sales presentation, 101

Index

see Interactive
Sample selection, 34-35
Sampling, 55
    rate, 56
Scanned images/documents, 168
Scanner data analysis (SDA), 149-152
    benefits, 150
    description, 149-150
    software, marketing/sales applications, 150
SCANTRACK, 151
Scheduling, 64, 71, 101
Screen
    dimmers, 5
    files, 142
    flexibility, 35
Scripting, 96
    language, 43
SDA, *see* Scanner
Search-and-replace function, 112
Security, 92
Segments, 135, 136
Senior executives, 4
Service, 12, 18
    see Product/service
    company, 31
SFA, *see* Sales force
Sharp Wizard, 63, 198
SIC, *see* Standard Industrial Classification
SIG, *see* Special interest group
Site
    selection, 84
    type, 36
Slide mode, 109
Smith Kline Beecham, 43
Software, 11, 35, 116, 167-176
    see Accounting, Calculating, Character, Communications, Contact, Database, Dedicated, DOS, Electronic bulletin, Executive, Fax, Financial management, Front-end, Groupware, List, Mailing list, Mapping, Menu-driven, Multimedia, OCR, Presentation, Project,

Record-keeping, Scanner, Spreadsheet, Stand-alone, Stock, Survey, Telecommunications, Text, Textbase, Timekeeping, Utility, Voice mail
    applications, 23, 85
    benefits, 6
    consultant, 6
    description, 6
    developer, 75
    export, 37
    file translation, 111
    integration, 28-29
    marketplace, 6
    package, 3, 7
    planner, 65
    publisher, 8
    selection, 10
    superstores, 7
    trends, 204-206
Sonar Professional, 169
Sort flexibility, 35
Spatial analysis tools, 84
Special interest groups (SIGs), 123
Special-interest magazines, 31
Spelling checkers, 24-25, 29, 44, 110
Spreadsheet(s), 28, 47, 77, 101, 113-119, 139, 150, 180, 181, 185
    benefits, 114
    capacity, 116
    case study, 116
    computations, 117
    customizability, 116
    description, 113
    ease, 116
    formatting, 116
    marketing/sales applications, 114-116
    software, selection, 116-117
    speed, 116
Stand-alone
    desktop computer, 100
    package, 100, 150
    software, 76, 150
Standard Industrial Classification code, 36

SIC, 36, 38
Statistical functions, 138
Statistics, 35
    see Built-in, Summary
Stock trading software, 32
Store and forward, 91
Strategic planning, 101
Strategy, formulation, 191
Street-based mapping, 84
Structured information, 69
Style
    see Type size/style
    sheet, 23, 29
Sub-notebook computers, 75
Summary
    list statistics, 35, 36
    report, 73
    statistics, 32
Support, 18, 108
Survey (software), 140
Survey(s), 49-50, 58
    see Mail
    analysis, 114
    data, 114, 143
    design, 135
Survey software, 135-140, 180
    description, 135-137
    marketing/sales applications, 137-138
    selection, 138
Synergy, 212
System operator (Sysop), 171

T

Tab settings, 23
TabHouse, 138-140
Table
    see Data, Query
    filters, 140
Tabulation, 135
    see Cross-tabulation
Taligent, 202
Target list, generation, 125
Target marketing, 84
    system, 17
Technical support, 17

Technology
    see Computer, Corporate, Emerging, Hardware, Information, Microcomputer, Pen, Pen-based, Tool
    benefits, measurement, 189-190
    cost, measurement, 189
    tools, 22-176
    tool application, 181-216
Telecommunications
    hardware, 76
    package
        ease, 96
        selection, 96
    protocol, 76
    software, 76
TeleForm, 50, 52, 137
Telemarketing, 17, 50, 101, 181-182
    support, see Inbound, Outbound
Telephone Consumer Protection Act of 1991, 49, 58
Template, 28, 42, 70, 104, 109, 111, 112, 115
    flexibility, 72
Test-market data, 17
Text retrieval, 167-169, 181
Text retieval software
    benefits, 168-169
    description, 167-168
    marketing/sales applications, 169
Text search, 167
Textbase software, 167
Thematic mapping, 83
Theoretical models, use, 18
Thesaurus(es), 25, 29
Thought processing software
    benefits, 166
    description, 165-166
    marketing/sales applications, 166
Thought processor(s), 165-167, 181
TIGER, see Topologically
Time (magazine), 40
Time management software
    benefits, 64
    description, 63
    marketing/sales applications, 64-65

Index

selection, 65
Time managers, 63-68, 183, 184
Timekeepers, 159-164
Timekeeping software
  benefits, 160
  description, 160
  marketing/sales applications, 161
Timeline, 162, 164
Timeslips, 162-163, 164
Tool
  see Spatial, Technology
  application, 177-216
    future direction, 207-216
    future technologies, 197-206
  bar, 29
Topologically Integrated Geographic Encoding and Referencing, 86
TIGER, 86
Training, 18, 43
  materials, creation, 26
Type
  setting, 39-41, 44
  size/style, 23, 139
Typeface, 23, 29

U

Uncertainty, 194
Universal Product Code (UPC), 16
UNIX, 7
Unstructure information, 69
UPC, *see* Universal Product Code
U.S. Census Bureau, 86
User
  see End, Personal computer
  directories, 92
  interface, 9, 10, 95, 204-205
  passwords, 92
  reaction evaluation, 137
User-definable icons, 73
User-defined field, 35, 69, 73
Utility software, 5

V

Value
  see Information, Potential

communication, 188
Value-added reseller (VAR), 75
VAR, *see* Value-added
Vendors, 10, 32, 93, 95
Vertical applications, 104, 198, 205
Video, 156
  see Portable
  catalogs, 155
VideoSpigot, 156
Virtual
  focal point, 213
  office, 102
  reality, 200
Virus trappers, 5
Voice mail, 55-62, 92
  benefits, 57
  case study, 58-59
  compatibility, 59
  ease, 57, 59
  electronic mail comparison, 94
  flexibility, 57
  marketing/sales applications, 57-58
  operator drop ability, 59
  prompt shortcut ability, 59
  quality, 57
  selection, 59
  software, description, 55-56
  systems, 57
Voice mailbox, 56
Voice recognition, 198

W

WAN, *see* Wide area network
Weighted relevance, 168
Wide area network (WAN), 99, 201
Windows, 7, 9, 10, 40, 45, 72, 97, 104, 105, 111, 117, 123, 143, 154, 156, 161, 162, 202, 204
  Teleform, 52
  user, 4
WinFaxPro, 52
Wire, The, 97, 98
Word
  see Microsoft
  formatting, 23

Word processing/processor, 23-30, 47,
77, 102, 109, 139, 150, 182
   marketing/sales applications, 26-27
   programs, 44
   selection, 28-29
   sofytware, 69, 104
      description, 23-26
Work flow automation, 100
Work group computer applications, 99

Work-group
   DTP, 40
   feature, 104
Worksheets, 13

X

Xerox, 204